Football is the very fabric of our nation. It bonds family members of all ages and people of all races.

Choo Seng Quee

Singapore must learn how to play with a nationalistic spirit like wild-fire with emotion and with a real determination to win.

Choo Seng Quee

Uncle Choo Seng Quee was the greatest football coach Singapore has ever produced; the best talent scout in Asia; and the soccer saviour of our two closest neighbours, Malaysia and Indonesia.

Jeffrey Low
Former The Straits Times *journalist*

Soccer is my life. It will end in soccer.

Choo Seng Quee

UNCLE CHOO

Singapore's Greatest Football Coach

UNCLE CHOO

Singapore's Greatest Football Coach

Foreword by
Ambassador Tommy Koh

REYNOLD GODWIN PEREIRA

World Scientific

NEW JERSEY · LONDON · SINGAPORE · BEIJING · SHANGHAI · HONG KONG · TAIPEI · CHENNAI · TOKYO

Published by

World Scientific Publishing Co. Pte. Ltd.

5 Toh Tuck Link, Singapore 596224

USA office: 27 Warren Street, Suite 401-402, Hackensack, NJ 07601

UK office: 57 Shelton Street, Covent Garden, London WC2H 9HE

National Library Board, Singapore Cataloguing in Publication Data
Name(s): Pereira, Reynold Godwin.
Title: Uncle Choo : Singapore's greatest football coach / Reynold Godwin Pereira ;
    foreword by Ambassador Tommy Koh.
Description: Singapore : World Scientific Publishing Co. Pte. Ltd., [2023]
Identifier(s): ISBN 978-981-12-6847-2 (hardback) | 978-981-12-6945-5 (paperback) |
    978-981-12-6848-9 (ebook for institutions) | 978-981-12-6849-6 (ebook for individuals)
Subject(s): LCSH: Soccer coaches--Singapore--Biography. | Soccer--Coaching--Singapore. |
    Soccer--Singapore--History.
Classification: DDC 796.334092--dc23

British Library Cataloguing-in-Publication Data
A catalogue record for this book is available from the British Library.

For any available supplementary material, please visit
https://www.worldscientific.com/worldscibooks/10.1142/13203#t=suppl

Desk Editor: Jiang Yulin

Typeset by Stallion Press
Email: enquiries@stallionpress.com

Printed in Singapore

For my wife, Karine and my sons, Raphaël and Tristan
In memory of my late mother, Soosana Lily Pereira

About the Author

Reynold Pereira was born in Singapore in 1964. He sat at the gallery stands with his father cheering on the Singapore national football team during the glorious 1970s, first at the Jalan Besar Stadium and then at the old National Stadium. He played football himself and trained with the Singapore Under-16 B team preparing for the Lion City Cup in 1979. But he did not make it into the final squad. He represented the Singapore Law Society veterans football team at the Lawyers World Cup in Alicante, Spain in 2008. He is a qualified non-practicing lawyer. He now lives in Barcelona, Spain with his wife and spends his weekends cheering on his two boys who both play amateur football for local Spanish clubs. In his remaining spare time, he still plays football with a local veterans' team. He also sings in a band. He is the founder of the Facebook page, 'Nostalgic Singapore'. This is his first book.

Contents

F o r e w o r d

ootball is the world's most popular team sport. Once every four years, the best 32 national teams of the world meet to compete for the FIFA World Cup. The latest edition was held in Qatar in 2022. The FIFA World Cup attracts a larger audience than the Olympic Games.

Football is not just a spectator sport. A good national team can evoke in the spectators, strong feelings of patriotism, pride and unity. Older Singaporeans, like me, still remember the pride which Singaporeans had in our national team, during the 1960s, 1970s and 1980s. When our team played against teams from Malaysia, the "Kallang Roar" by our spectators would intimidate our opponents and inspire our team.

The situation today is quite sad. Our national team is ranked by FIFA at 160. We have never qualified to play at the FIFA World Cup tournament. Attendances for S.League matches are in the hundreds.

How to produce a great football team? One of the answers is the coach. It is for this reason that I welcome Reynold Godwin Pereira's initiative to write a book about Choo Seng Quee, popularly known as Uncle Choo. One of our best sports journalists, Jeffrey Low, has described Uncle Choo as the greatest football coach Singapore has produced.

Uncle Choo was the coach of the Singapore team which won the Malaysia Cup, in 1964, 1965 and 1977. He would not have been appointed as the coach in 1977 if not for the strong support of N. Ganesan, the Chairman of the Football Association of Singapore. Ganesan believed in Uncle Choo and protected him from the interference of ignorant football officials. Singapore needs football officials like Mr Ganesan.

What made Uncle Choo such a great coach?

First, he had an encyclopedia knowledge of the game. Second, he was passionate about football from a very young age. He talked football, dreamt football and was obsessive about football. Third, he was able to spot talent and was prepared to spend years mentoring the talented young players. Fourth, he believed in a military-style training regime. His players were physically fit and mentally strong.

Fifth, he was able to unite players, of different races, into a solid and harmonious team. Sixth, he took care of his players and would help individual players with their problems. The players knew that he was fierce but kind. Seventh, he instilled national pride in all his players. At every training session, he would make them sing the national anthem, with gusto. He would make them sign the anthem again and again until he was satisfied.

Eighth, he had courage. During the final of the Malaysia Cup in 1977, he noticed that the captain of the team, Samad Allapitchay, was not playing well. At half time, Uncle Choo took the bold step of dropping Samad from the team. During the second half, Uncle Choo also replaced another player, S. Rajagopal. The two moves were correct, and the team defeated Penang by three goals to two in overtime. The hero of the match was Quah Kim Song. He headed in the decisive third goal.

If Singapore football is to progress, we need officials like N. Ganesan and coaches like Uncle Choo. We should remember and celebrate the life of Uncle Choo, Singapore's greatest football coach.

Professor Tommy Koh
Ambassador-at-Large
Ministry of Foreign Affairs
Singapore

P r e f a c e

It is almost noon. The midday heat beats down on the Choa Chu Kang Christian Cemetery. In land hungry Singapore, it is the only remaining active cemetery. The meteorological station had forecasted another hot and humid day (no surprise here!). The scorching heat forces even the insects to scamper for any cool spots they can find.

But one Indian gentleman ignores the blistering heat. He patiently cleans a pearl white tomb. This Indian man is in his mid-60s but is still in great physical condition. Drops of sweat drip from all sides of his slight frame. Using his bare hands, he endeavours to remove the weeds protruding from the sides of the gleaming white tomb.

This tombstone belongs to a Chinese man. Despite being exposed to the elements of nature for almost 40 years, it still looks in pristine condition. The Indian man cleans the beautiful Madonna and child headstone and removes all traces of dirt and grime from the tomb.

After almost one hour, he is finally done. He gently lays several stalks of fresh flowers into two vases at the base of the tomb. He then places a polystyrene cup containing some 'teh susu' (tea with milk) on the tomb. With his head bowed, he prays silently for a few minutes. He then removes the polystyrene cup before silently walking off. He has been faithfully exercising this monthly ritual (whenever he is in town) for the past 35 years, come rain or shine.

The Indian man is former Singapore football star, R. Suria Murthi. Suria Murthi or 'Suria' as he is affectionately known to his friends and adorning fans, was discovered by this Chinese man when he was a skinny 12-year-old boy running around Farrer Park with a football at his feet. The Chinese man made him juggle the ball from 3pm to 5pm every day for a couple of years.

By age 16, Suria had represented Singapore Indians and was captain of the Tampines Rovers Football Club youth team. Suria went on to play for Singapore from 1977 to 1991. He then headed north and represented states in the Malaysia Cup. He is the proud owner of the record of playing for the most number of Malaysian clubs in the 1990s.

And the Chinese man whose tomb Suria has been faithfully looking after all these years is none other than Choo Seng Quee. He passed away in 1983.

Many Singaporeans no longer recognise this name. The stories of his life have been stored away in some decaying folders in some dark and dusty shelves. But for some die hard Singaporean, Malaysian and Indonesian football fans who have followed football closely in the second half of the 20th century, especially from 1950 to 1980, his name shines like a beacon of light. The mere mention of his name conjures up images of a golden era when South-east Asian football stood on par with the best that Asia could offer. (I myself was fortunate to learn about Seng Quee from my cousin, Jerome Vaz, when I was in my early teens. My cousin, together with some other young teenagers, trained under Seng Quee in Farrer Park around 1976.)

Choo Seng Quee or 'Uncle Choo' as he was affectionately known to his players and fans alike, was one of the most colourful and controversial figures that Singapore has ever produced. Many in Singapore acknowledge him as the greatest football coach that Singapore ever had. His greatness is also recognised by fans from Malaya (later reconstituted as Malaysia) and Indonesia when he coached their respective teams during the 1950s and 1960s.

In Singapore, he produced teams made up of multiracial players who set aside their racial differences and played for the national flag. His superb command of Malay, owing to his Peranakan background, aided him in his communication with his players.

Many adjectives have been used to describe this football 'maverick' who always wanted to have things done his way. Jeffrey Low, a former newspaper journalist, called him a 'moralist, educationist, wicked sergeant-major, preacher, singer, orator, leader, cry-baby, fighter, and philanthropist' all rolled into one.

Percy Seneviratne, another former newspaper journalist, described him as being a combination of former volatile Brazilian football coach, Saldanha (who was in charge of the Brazilian team for the qualifying matches for the 1970 World Cup and had once brandished a revolver when confronting a critic, though I doubt Seng Quee ever went that far!) and Percy Cerutty (the equally controversial Australian athletics coach who pioneered a home-spun system of 'Stotan' training, embracing a holistic regime of natural diets, hard training in natural surroundings, and mental stimulation).

He was brought up in a Singapore that was slowly recovering from the ashes of the First World War. He came from a generation where coaching was very rudimentary, where the favoured method of training was without the football. It was an era before professional football, where the game was played for the love of it and not for financial gain. His was a world where budgets were tiny and where balanced diets were not introduced into the training arena and where it was not unheard of to see his players eating local fare at roadside stalls.

At times, though, his too rigid, almost military-like training methods was not well-received by his trainees but more often than not, it brought great success to the teams that he coached. Some of his methods were so radical it is said that you are either for him or you hate him. He had his loyal followers as well as those who had nothing good to say about him.

But when it came to vision and coaching methods, he was way ahead of everyone during his time. So much so that in 1959, Jimmy McIlroy who was at that time playing for Burnley Football Club, the reigning English league champions, decided to adopt Seng Quee's diet method of eating more carbohydrates rather than solely relying on proteins which was the favoured diet regime of English footballers.

His coaching prowess was recognised as early as 1952 when one journalist referred to him as Singapore's greatest authority on football.

But it was beyond the shores of Singapore that he forged his reputation as a master tactician. Seng Quee spent the decade and a half from 1950 to 1964 establishing a reputation as one of the foremost coaches in South-east Asia. His reputation was forged training both the Indonesian national team and the Malaysian national team.

Sadly, his direct 'no nonsense' manner and at times, almost crude mannerism, meant that he was almost at constant 'war' with the football administrators in Singapore. He was never afraid of expressing himself and in some instances, throwing tantrums when things were not right. He had no qualms about having direct confrontations with the sporting authorities especially when it involved his players' welfare. In my interviews with several ex-national players, many agreed that he always stood by his players when he felt that they were unjustly dealt with.

A case in point was when he voiced his displeasure over the suspension of former Singapore star striker Quah Kim Song in 1975 for alleged insubordination.

This uneasy and often fragile relationship with the football bureaucrats in Singapore meant that his opportunities to coach the Singapore national team were limited.

During a coaching career that stretched nearly four decades, Seng Quee had only five relatively short stints as Singapore coach, some lasting for only a few months. His first experience happened a couple of months before his 35th birthday in 1949. His second stint as Singapore coach came almost 15 years later in 1964 in the midst of a rather troubled time in Singapore's history.

Singapore was in the midst of an unhappy union with the Federation of Malaysia. The tensions boiled over culminating in racial riots and eventually Singapore's departure from the Federation of Malaysia in 1965.

But, in spite of this disruptive period, he famously led the Singapore team to successive victories in the Malaya Cup in 1964 and 1965.

But for all his achievements, it is sad that Seng Quee has never been given the credit that he truly deserved in Singapore. His path mirrored that of some of the earlier coaches in English football like Jimmy Hogan and George Raynor who found more success outside their home countries than within their homeland.

(Jimmy Hogan coached teams in the Netherlands, Austria, Hungary, Switzerland and Germany. He is sometimes credited with the revolution in European football that saw Hungary thrash

England 6-3 at Wembley in 1953, ushering in a new football era. Meanwhile, George Raynor led the Swedish national team to the final of the 1958 World Cup. The English Football Association sadly never really recognised their achievements.)

Seng Quee is typical in many ways, because his reputation remains considerably higher abroad than at home.

Both Indonesia and Malaysia spared no efforts in rewarding him for his valuable services to football in their respective countries.

For his contribution to the development of Indonesian football, the Indonesian Football Federation conferred upon Seng Quee the First Class Gold Medal at a special ceremony in Jakarta to commemorate the 50th anniversary of the Indonesian Football Federation in 1982.

The Malaysians acknowledged his achievements of the late 1950s by sending him on a six-month overseas attachment to the UK to study modern methods of coaching and training in 1961. He spent six months with three English clubs, first, with Burnley, the reigning English champions, followed by Everton and Sheffield United. (Imagine one of our Singapore coaches being sent to Manchester City to work closely with Pep Guardiola today!)

He had a special bond with Tunku Abdul Rahman, the Malaysian Prime Minister (who was also the President of the Football Association of Malaysia [FAM]). So tight was their relationship that the Tunku kept him at the helm of the Malaysian team from 1958 to 1964. Had it not been for Seng Quee's determination in wanting to return to coach his motherland, the Tunku would most certainly have kept Seng Quee as Malaysian coach for a much longer period.

His recognition in Singapore only came after his success in winning the Malaysia Cup for Singapore in 1977. The Singapore

National Olympic Council (SNOC) awarded the Coach of the Year award to him in 1977.

For many Singaporeans, that victory in the 1977 Malaysia Cup Final was his greatest achievement. This ended a barren spell of 12 years without victory in the Malaysia Cup. For others, Seng Quee's 'magnum opus' was his success in the 1977 pre-World Cup qualifying competition. During this memorable tournament, Singapore marched all the way to the final. They swept aside the perennial South-east Asian giants like Thailand and tournament hot favourites, Malaysia. They only stumbled at the final hurdle, narrowly losing to the professionals from Hong Kong in a close final.

As a person, he touched the lives of many people. Those who worked closely with him in his coaching staff fondly remember him as a caring person who looked after their needs and always went out of his way to ensure that they were treated properly and he sometimes paid them extra from his own pocket.

Many will be surprised to know that he also excelled as a player. He played a pivotal role as a promising tough defender in the Straits Chinese Football Association (SCFA) team. His impressive performances with SCFA, aided by his unlimited energy and skills, resulted in him donning the Singapore colours. Sadly, his playing career was cut short by the Second World War. While playing for Chinese Athletic Association in 1939, he decided to try his hand at coaching at the tender age of 35. Thus, this began a coaching career that lasted for more than 40 years until his death in 1983.

The reasons behind my writing the life story of such a gifted footballer, coach and remarkable character are simple. I felt that his story needed to be told, especially to the newer generation.

Many Singapore fans today lament the fact that football in Singapore is in the doldrums. The historians add that the current level of football in Singapore is not what you would expect from a nation with a strong football tradition stretching back to the turn of the 20th century.

But, there was, in fact, a time when Singapore stood side by side with other South-east Asian powerhouses like Malaysia, Thailand and Myanmar. And that achievement can be attributed to one man who raised a team driven by traditional values like hard work and discipline; a team that was able to outrun and outlast other teams. And he managed to achieve success with a multiracial Singaporean team who set aside any racial differences to play for the Singapore flag.

Many people adopt romantic notions of people especially after they have passed on to the next world. I have been accused of portraying an idealised view of the legend especially since I have not met Uncle Choo in person. However, after speaking to many former national players who had trained under him and having read many articles praising his football acumen, I am convinced that he has made a positive contribution to football both in Singapore and South-east Asia in general. History has proven the genius in Uncle Choo if we consider his achievements as a coach with Indonesia, Malaysia and Singapore.

This book is my tribute to this wonderful and colourful person. It is my hope that it will help the younger generation realise that we can produce quality homegrown coaches especially if they were given the right opportunities and encouraged to put forth their ideas to raise the standard of Singapore football.

For this book, I tried to speak to as many people as possible who had the honour of playing under him and have had first-hand experience of his wisdom. It was a race against the clock as some of his football 'sons' have passed on to the next world!

Many ex-national players and coaches were more than happy to share experiences, both positive and negative of this enigma of a person.

For others who have already passed on, like Dollah Kassim, Majid Ariff and N. Ganesan, I'm glad that there are audio recordings from the National Archives of Singapore where significant portions of their interviews touched on how Seng Quee created a huge impact on the development of football in the South-east Asian region.

I hope that you will enjoy reading this book about this legend. In the words of former *Straits Times* journalist Jeffrey Low (who has written many articles about Seng Quee and had followed Seng Quee's career very closely during the 1970s):

> "*Uncle Choo Seng Quee was the greatest football coach Singapore has ever produced; the best talent scout in Asia, and the soccer saviour of our two closest neighbours, Malaysia and Indonesia.*"

P r o l o g u e

Crowning Glory

Merdeka Stadium, Kuala Lumpur, 28 May 1977

The setting — the final of the Malaysia Cup football final between Singapore and Penang.

Ninety minutes of fast and furious football had been produced in the incessant rain. The teams were deadlocked at 1-1. Referee Koh Guan Kiat from Selangor blew the whistle for full-time. Extra time was needed to try to separate these two titans in Malaysia Cup football.

The coaching staff spent the few minutes before extra time massaging the tired legs of the players to prepare them for another 30 minutes of battle. Coach Seng Quee was busy shouting last-minute words of encouragement to his 'boys'. He knew it was going to be tough. But deep down, he was confident. He had prepared his players both physically and mentally for this moment. The players had gone through weeks of brutal physical training in almost military-like conditions. Strict dietary regimes were implemented by Seng Quee. The players were made to sleep together in dormitories.

And yes, the sacrifices paid off. The Singapore team overcame the clearly exhausted Penang team in extra-time to lift the much treasured Malaysia Cup.

Seng Quee had done what many coaches, both local and foreign, brought in by the Football Association of Singapore, had strived but failed to do; bring home the Malaysia Cup after an absence of 12 years.

The name Choo Seng Quee conjures up different images for different people. For some, he is the elder statesman affectionately known as 'Uncle Choo' with his words of wisdom. For others, he is a tyrant known to punish players by making them go through tough routines during training and being too much of a 'nanny' figure in the way he tried to control them during their overseas tours.

For others like R. Suria Murthi, former left half or left winger in the Singapore team and many other clubs, Seng Quee made them what they are; great players with the intelligence and the ability to play top-level football.

To better understand how this man managed to unite teams, we will have to explore the different facets of this legendary man, of what made him tick and how he became the legend that he is.

Chapter One

The Turbulent Sixties

To understand a little bit more about Choo Seng Quee, we need to first, turn back to a turbulent chapter in Singapore's history. For many, the 1960s conjures up vivid images of a world in full swing; the mini skirts, the Cuban missile crisis, the assassination of President John F. Kennedy of the United States of America, the Beatles, and later in the decade, the mods, and the hippies.

For Singapore, the 1960s proved to be a critical period in its history. Post-war Singapore introduced a new breed of intellectuals who felt that the British had overstayed their welcome. Efforts were made to gain independence. After an unsuccessful attempt by Chief Minister David Marshall in 1955, self-independence from the British was finally granted in 1959. The People's Action Party (PAP) led by a young and ambitious lawyer, won 43 seats out of 51 to form the new government. Lee Kuan Yew became Prime Minister but control of his party was shared with populists on the left and the right.

The early 1960s saw internal bickering between those two camps in the PAP which reached a boiling point in 1961 when 13 PAP assemblymen from the left were expelled from the party. This led to a split in the newly formed PAP government resulting in the creation of the Barisan Sosialis.

Then, following a referendum in 1963, Malaysia was formed on 16 September 1963 in the merger of the Federation of Malaya with the former British colonies of North Borneo, Sarawak and Singapore. This significant date marked the end of a 144-year British rule in Singapore which began with the founding of modern Singapore by Sir Stamford Raffles in 1819.

Not surprisingly, this fragile merger lasted for a mere 24 months. From the initiation of the merger, cracks already started to appear owing to distrust and ideological differences between the leaders of Singapore and their counterparts from the federal government of Malaysia.

This unstable period saw riots taking place in July and September 1964 — the worst riots Singapore had experienced since the end of the Second World War. The riots were sparked by racial tensions between the Chinese and the Malays which were fuelled by rising tensions between the PAP government in Singapore and Malaysia's ruling Alliance Party, a coalition led by the United Malays National Organisation.

To avoid any further racial conflict, Prime Minister Tunku Abdul Rahman decided that Singapore should separate from Malaysia. Despite last-ditch attempts by PAP leaders, including Lee Kuan Yew, to keep Singapore as a state in the union, the Malaysian Parliament on 9 August 1965 voted 126-0 in favour of the separation of Singapore, with Members of Parliament from Singapore not present during the voting.

Hence on 9 August 1965, a tearful Lee proclaimed and declared that Singapore was a sovereign, independent nation and assumed the role of Prime Minister of the new nation.

Eight days before that fateful day, a slightly overweight Chinese man (who would later be synonymous with his batik shirt) called

Choo Seng Quee proudly led a multiracial Singapore national team to victory in the illustrious Malaya Cup, retaining the trophy that Singapore had won the year before.

It was an immense achievement. Even with the unstable situation and uneasy air surrounding Singapore and the Malaysian Peninsula, Seng Quee had raised a team which overcame racial barriers and lifted the Malaya Cup both in 1964 and 1965.

Of course, Singapore had multiracial squads before who were also successful in the Malaya/Malaysia Cup. So, why were his achievements any different from those of his predecessors? For a start, he was from a rare breed of coaches who managed to instil a sense of pride and loyalty in his team. For him, a player's ethnic background was not the determining factor. It was their ability to play as a team and set aside any racial differences that mattered more. And he achieved success in the midst of strong racial tensions culminating in racial riots which had threatened to divide an already fragile region even more.

His appointment in 1964 came on the back of a successful six-year adventure with the Malayan team. The highlight during this successful period was a bronze medal in the Asian Games in 1962. The Tunku in Malaysia was prepared to extend his contract in 1964. But Seng Quee's dream had always been to elevate the status of football of his place of birth.

And before that successful spell with Singapore's perennial rivals from the north, he did a marvellous job in turning previous 'minnows' Indonesia into a force to be reckoned with, especially after their successes in Hong Kong against several reputable sides. (We will come to that later.)

He enjoyed his coaching stints in Malaysia and Indonesia which gave him the opportunity to train players of different cultures and backgrounds. However, those close to him knew that though his heart was always with Singapore. He had expressed his desire on numerous occasions to train the Singapore team and raise the level of the game in Singapore.

Sadly for Singapore football, after that Malaya Cup success in 1965, the trophy cabinet in the Singapore Amateur Football Association (SAFA) would remain empty for 12 long years. It was only in 1977 that Singapore recaptured the Malaysia Cup. Once again, it was under the masterful guidance of Seng Quee.

Seng Quee did have several other opportunities to train the Singapore team in the 1960s but these stints would be short and often dominated by off-the-field bickering between Seng Quee and SAFA.

But who this man really is? What was it that made him into a great coach with the ability to get the best from his players? Perhaps it may be appropriate to step into a time machine and travel back to start from the very beginning of Seng Quee's life. But it would also be appropriate to understand a little about the development of Singapore football from the early days to fully appreciate his formative years.

Chapter Two

Dawn of Football in Singapore

Seng Quee made his grand entry into the Singapore football scene in the early 1930s. By then, competitive football was already well established in the then British colony with domestic league and cup competitions and the ever-growing Malaya Cup already into its second decade.

Football has always been the people's game in Singapore. It is hard to imagine that football was not played in Singapore before the British arrived in 1819.

When discussing the origins of football in Singapore and Malaysia, it is vital to draw up a distinction between the game as we know it today and any sport that involves using one's feet to kick a ball. If we are talking purely about the latter, it is quite probable that it was played even before the historic landing of Sir Stamford Raffles.

Fédération Internationale de Football Association (FIFA), the world governing body for football, has recognised that the first indications of an early formal form of football date back 3,000 years to Ancient China. By 50 AD, the game was named tsu 'chu' (or 'cuju'). The Chinese artist Du Jin, who was active between 1465 and 1509, painted three ladies playing 'cuju' in a garden. This was during the

Ming Dynasty which saw the Chinese adopt an expansionist policy. Sea voyages were made by the eunuch Admiral Zheng He to Southeast Asia. Yet, no evidence exists of 'cuju' being brought to Southeast Asia.

There is evidence though that another form of ball game did exist in Malaysia before the British arrived. According to the Sejarah Melayu (Malay Annals), during the 15th century, there was an incident of Raja Muhammad, a son of Sultan Mansur Shah who was accidentally hit with a rattan ball by Tun Besar, a son of Tun Perak, in a sepak raga game. Sepak raja or 'sepak takraw' as it is more popularly known is played with a rattan ball which is passed on using any part of the body except lower arms and hands.

The modern game of football is popularly accredited to the British especially with the introduction of the rules of association football. The British brought the game to the colonies and Singapore and Malaya were no exception.

With the advent of association football, teams were formed among the expatriates working in the British companies that were set up in Singapore. Teams with links to the British military also sprang up in Singapore. And added to that, some social clubs that were catered to the expatriates also formed their own football teams.

One of the earliest teams to be formed from the social clubs was the Singapore Cricket Club (SCC). It was originally founded in 1852 and the original members were mostly men working in the British business and mercantile community, usually as clerks or 'junior assistants'. The SCC football team was created in the 1880s and dominated the local football scene during the early years winning the SAFA league four years consecutively from 1911 to 1914.

The SCC and the Singapore Recreation Club (SRC was founded in 1883 to cater to the Eurasians in Singapore) played their home games at the Padang, an open playing field located within the heart of the commercial centre in Singapore. The area was once known as 'Raffles Plain'.

Though the rules of association football were introduced in 1863, organised football was played in Singapore as early as 1849. *The Singapore Free Press and Mercantile Advertiser* dated 4 January 1849 recorded a football match taking place on New Year's Day of that year at the Esplanade. We can only speculate that it consisted of a mixture of the 'dribbling' game (association football) and the 'handling' game (rugby).

Another article in *The Singapore Free Press* dated 25 January 1866 described a football match that took place between the Officers of the Royal Artillery and Navy and some locals. It is not clear whether that game was played according to the rules of association football which were codified three years earlier in 1863 by the Football Association (FA) in England. The article strangely mentioned that football was a game where every advantage obtained over your opponents was deemed as fair, such as tripping up and running away with the ball.

It was in the public schools in the UK that the modern game with its standard set of rules was shaped. An old Salopian from Cambridge University, John Charles Thring drew up a list of 10 rules in 1862. He drew up these rules for what he called the 'Simplest Game'.

In late 1863, the English FA was formed and adopted Thring's rules with some adjustments and elaborations. The FA decided to codify the rules and coin it as 'association football' to distinguish the game from the other forms of football played at the time, specifically rugby football.

There has been disputes as to when association football was first played in Singapore. In a *Straits Times* article dated 12 October 1894, it was mentioned that a certain Mr. Hornby was the first man to introduce association football in 1888. Hornby later became the captain of the SCC football team.

However, according to the book, *One Hundred Years of Singapore*, published in 1921, association football was first played in Singapore in 1889. That momentous occasion saw two teams of British engineers battle against each other on a grassy surface at Tank Road. The ground was in fact a cricket pitch belonging to the Police and it was known as the Police Cricket Ground. The ground was close to Messrs. Howarth, Erskine and Company, an engineering firm where most of the engineers probably worked. Later, the company merged with another engineering firm, Riley Hargreaves and Company, in 1912 to form United Engineers Limited which still exists today.

Two prominent figures during that era, Robert Scoular and James McKenzie sometimes played with the engineers. Scoular and McKenzie went on to form the SCC football team. The SCC football team were to emerge as a powerhouse in Singapore football during the period before and after the First World War. Robert Scoular later became the Chairman of John Little & Co., a firm which later sprouted Singapore's well-known department store — John Little's. James McKenzie started a dispensary firm called Singapore Dispensary.

Besides the engineers and SCC, there were also the military teams. With more and more teams being formed, friendly matches began to take place at several venues. There was a growing desire to have competitive matches and to have a governing body to be responsible for the organisation of these competitive games, hence the birth of the Singapore Football Association (SFA).

Singapore Football Association

The Singapore Football Association (SFA) was founded in 1892. It is believed to be the oldest football association in Asia. The Indian Football Association only came about a year later in 1893. The first President was William Edward Maxwell who was also then the acting Governor of the Straits Settlements.

The SFA underwent a name change in 1929 and became known as the Singapore Amateur Football Association (SAFA) to distinguish it from the Selangor Football Association (SFA). The current name, the Football Association of Singapore (FAS) came about on 13 January 1966.

Challenge Cup

One of the first tasks for the SFA was the organisation of the Challenge Cup. A meeting was held on 23 January 1892 where several parties expressed interest in creating a challenge cup competition. Eight teams registered for the first Challenge Cup. They were:
1. Royal Artillery
2. Singapore Cricket Club (SCC)
3. 58th Regiment (team one)
4. 58th Regiment (team two)
5. Raffles School
6. Royal Engineers
7. Engineers Association
8. Police

Each team was asked to contribute a sum of $10 towards the cup, and provide medals for members of the winning team.

The first Challenge Cup final saw the Engineers take on the Royal Artillery at the Esplanade. According to news reports, the weather was perfect for a final. Matches were normally played in the evenings where the weather was a little cooler. The Engineers came out victors by six goals to two.

The Engineers retained the Challenge Cup in 1893. Sadly, that was the last time they were to lay their hands on the trophy. From 1894 until the commencement of the First World War, the military teams dominated the competition. That run was only broken on two occasions by SCC who carried home the cup in 1901 and 1903.

The post-war period saw the rise of the 'local' teams and in 1925, the Straits Chinese Football Association (SCFA) became the first local Asian team to win the coveted trophy. They also captured the trophy on three occasions (1935, 1937 and 1939) during their golden era in the 1930s. It was during this wonderful period that Choo Seng Quee made his mark in the SCFA team as we shall see shortly.

(Note: Records also show another cup competition, the Warren Challenge Football Shield, debuting in 1894. The first winners were the Singapore Voluntary Artillery. They retained the shield in 1895.)

Singapore Football League

The first attempt to create a football league took place in January 1904. In his book, *Indiscreet Memories*, Edwin A. Brown recollected that a meeting was called (at the initiation of members from the Young Men's Christian Association [YMCA]) to discuss the idea of a football league. The suggestion was adopted. Twelve teams, mostly Europeans, registered for the first-ever league competition. The inaugural match of the newly formed Association Football League took place on 2 March 1904 between YMCA and Tanjong Pagar. Here is how *The Singapore Free Press and Mercantile*

Advertiser (Weekly) dated 3 March 1904 described the excitement surrounding this momentous match:

> *"The match had been well advertised, and excellent seating arrangements having been made, there was a very large attendance of Europeans, including quite a gathering of ladies. There were besides, many natives present. Arrangements had been made to formally start the league by the President opening the first game, and at 5 o'clock, Mr. Cuscaden kicked off amidst cheers."*

The Band and Drums team which comprised the 1st Battalion Manchester Regiment prevailed in the first league competition with an unbeaten record, winning 16 of their 22 games.

From its inception until the end of the First World War, competitive football in Singapore was dominated by the expatriate community, though the first league competition already saw three teams including one or two 'local' players in their line-ups. But it soon became clear that there was a growing number of talented 'locals' available to boost the strength of the expatriate teams. The expatriate colonial community were eager to incorporate more of these talented locals into their teams to secure greater 'bragging rights' in the Long Bar of the Raffles Hotel!

Communal football in Singapore

Football before the Second World War and the two decades after the war was played along communal lines. Apart from the British military teams and the social teams like the SCC and the SRC, the various races in Singapore (Chinese, Malay, Indian and Eurasian) played for teams within their own racial groups.

The ever increasing popularity of football among the non-Europeans especially the Chinese and Malays created a demand for non-European clubs. The SCFA was founded in 1911 while the Singapore Malay Football Club was established a year earlier in 1910.

However, these were not the oldest non-European clubs. The Straits Chinese National Football Association was formed in 1891 while the Darul Adab Club was formed in 1893 to cater for the Malay-Muslim community.

While the entry of these 'local' teams increased the number of teams participating in the SFA league, the expatriate teams from the British Forces and the SCC continued their dominance in both the league and cup competitions. This dominance was finally broken in 1925 when the SCFA won both the 1st Division league title and cup competitions. Then in 1930, the Malay Football Association (MFA) won their first-ever cup competition.

The third decade of the 20th century finally saw the end of European dominance in league football in Singapore with the SCFA and the MFA winning eight out of the 10 league competitions during that decade.

The reason for the rise in the dominance of local teams could perhaps be explained by the growing popularity of the sport among the locals. Football was a relatively inexpensive sport requiring only a football (in some cases, any soft rounded object) and not involving any other sport accessories unlike cricket and hockey. The introduction of the Malaya Cup competition in 1921 also fuelled the sport's popularity among the locals. This competition gave the platform for local players to pit their skills against the best players from the various states in Malaya (before it became Malaysia in 1957). A little bit more about the Malaya Cup now.

Malaya/Malaysia Cup

The Malaya Cup (or more correctly named as the HMS Malaya Cup and later to be called the Malaysia Cup) is a football competition that has thrilled football fans from both sides of the Causeway since its introduction in 1921. It has a very fascinating story as to its origins.

The HMS Malaya was a warship that had been presented to Britain by the rulers and people of the Federated Malay States (FMS). It was used in the First World War, most notably in the Battle of Jutland in 1916. The Battle of Jutland was hailed as the greatest naval battle of the First World War. The ship sailed into Port Swettenham on 17 January 1921 and was anchored for 10 days at port. This was the first time that the vessel had ever come to Malayan waters. The officers and crew were extended a welcome stay and provided with hospitality of the highest level while they were in Malaya.

In a message that was wired by the commander of the warship, Captain H. T. Butler, to the Chief Secretary in Kuala Lumpur, he spoke of the warm hospitality extended to him by the rulers and the people of the FMS.

The ship left Malaya on 25 January 1921 'with much regret but very happy memories'. As a token of gratitude for their welcome stay, Captain Butler and his crew presented two trophies for sports in Malaya: one for a rugby competition and one for a football competition.

While both the rugby and football competitions were played at state level and attracted a following, it was the football competition that captured the imagination of the general public and became one of the sporting highlights of the annual sporting calendar.

(Interesting fact: The trophy for the rugby competition was lost in 1942 during the Japanese Occupation but was eventually found in the jungle just outside of Kuala Lumpur in 1961!)

History was made on 20 August 1921 when the first Malaya Cup match was played with Selangor defeating Penang 5-1 in front of an estimated crowd of 5,000 in Kuala Lumpur.

The six teams participating in the inaugural Malaya Cup football competition were organised into two groups. Singapore was pitted in the South Zone group and were paired with Negri Sembilan and Malacca while the northern section comprised Selangor, Penang and Perak.

Each team played with each other in a single round-robin format. (A round-robin styled tournament is where teams play one another an equal number of times, accumulating points as they win [or none if they lose]. In a round-robin tournament, the team with the best record is the winner.) The winners of each group progressed into the final.

Singapore made their entrance into the Malaya Cup on 10 September 1921, running out 4-0 winners against Negri Sembilan at the Negri Sembilan Club.

Three weeks later, the Singapore team lined up at the first Malaya Cup final on 1 October 1921 at the Selangor Club field (now Merdeka Square). Their rivals, the Selangor team, were to become their nemesis over the years. In a tense final, Singapore ran out winners by two goals to one with C. M. Jamieson and S. H. Moss scoring for Singapore while Selangor's goal was scored by R. de Rozario.

The Singapore team that had the honour of being the first victors of the Malaya Cup that day comprised of the following players: Larkin (goalkeeper); Gale and Wheatley (defence); Cheong Chee Lim, Philips and Cushway (midfield); and Smith, Lingard, Jamieson, Moss and Power (forward).

A no-nonsense half-back (midfielder in today's terminology), Cheong Chee Lim had the distinction of being the first Chinese to play for Singapore in a Malaya Cup final match. He was to play in all finals during the 1920s with the exception of the 1924 final (when the Chinese team broke away from the governing local authority) and the 1928 final.

Singapore dominated the early years appearing in every cup final from 1921 to 1941 — winning the cup 12 times during this amazing run and sharing the cup on two occasions (with Selangor).

The only blemish for the Singapore team during this remarkable run was the humiliating 8-1 defeat by Selangor in the 1927 final. The headline in the *Malaya Tribune* ran 'Singapore Outplayed in Malaya Cup Final'. The article even suggested that the Selangor team could have won by a larger margin! These were the 'infamous' Singapore players who played in that disastrous final: Cherrington (SCC), Pennefather (SRC), Yeow Soon (SCFA), Kemat (Malays), Chee Lim (SCFA), Boon Lay (SCFA), Wan Puteh (Police), Un Sun (SCFA), Yong Liang (SCFA), A. Fattah (Malays), Smith (SCC). Reserves: Mun Fun (SCFA) and Mat Noor (Malays).

The finals held in Singapore before the Second World War took place at the Anson Road Football Stadium (originally called 'Singapore Stadium').

Anson Stadium

The Anson Road Stadium, which was once described as the 'Wembley of Malaya', was a key venue for football in Singapore during the 1920s and 1930s. It was initially designed as the centrepiece for the Malaya-Borneo Exhibition in 1922, but subsequently became the home of competitive association football in Singapore. It hosted domestic league, tour and Malaya Cup matches from 1924 to 1941.

The stadium hosted its first HMS Malaya Cup final in 1925 with entrance charges at 20 cents, 50 cents and $1.22. (By 1941, the stadium charged around 50 cents to $2 for a football match.)

Interest in the Malaya Cup continued to soar and in 1933, a crowd of 10,000 packed the Anson Road Stadium to see Singapore record the biggest Malaya Cup win — an 8-2 demolition of Selangor with Singapore striker Chia Keng Hock bagging a hat-trick.

The rivalry between Singapore and Selangor (Malaya's version of the 'El Clasico' game featuring Spanish rivals, Real Madrid and Barcelona) would continue until the final decade of the 20th century when Singapore was eventually barred from taking part in subsequent competitions in 1994. This paved the way for Selangor to extend their domination in the Malaysia Cup. However, it also enabled other less successful teams like Perlis, Negri Sembilan and Kelantan to lay their hands on the trophy over the last 20 years.

In 1941, Singapore beat Selangor 2-1 to become the first team to win the trophy three times in a row. That would sadly be the last cup final for the next seven years as the Second World War put a halt to all sporting activities in Singapore and Malaya.

Many Singapore players (especially the expatriate players) traded their football gear for military outfits. Tragically, many players did not live to see the resumption of the Malaya Cup competition in 1948.

When the competition resumed in 1948, there were some new faces. Teams from Pahang, Kelantan, Terengganu and Perlis made their debut in the competition. The Singapore team did not fare as well as they had hoped for. They succumbed to eventual winners

Negri Sembilan during the group stages. For Negri Sembilan, it was their first Malaya Cup success since the inception of the tournament 27 years ago.

Seng Quee's first appointment as coach of the Singapore team came in 1949. SAFA gave him a four-month contract. Such short-term contracts were the norm during that period. His task was to lift the Malaya Cup for Singapore. Sadly, that was not to be the case. But more of that later.

The 1950s saw the continued supremacy of Singapore and Selangor though a short era of dominance by the Penang team saw them lifting the trophy three times during that decade.

In 1957, the final was played for the first time at the newly constructed Merdeka Stadium. The Merdeka Stadium had the added significance as the site of the formal declaration of independence of the Federation of Malaya on 31 August 1957 and it was the first modern building of the new nation. When it was completed, the stadium held the world record for the tallest pre-stressed floodlight towers and the biggest cantilever shell roofs. It was also the largest stadium in South-east Asia at the time of completion.

The Merdeka Stadium hosted the majority of the cup finals until the late 1990s. Since then, most of the finals have been held at the impressive Bukit Jalil National Stadium in Kuala Lumpur. This magnificent stadium which was built in 1998 can accommodate around 87,000 people. There were also a couple of finals held at the Shah Alam Stadium in Selangor during the second decade of the 21st century.

By the 1960s, 15 teams participated regularly in what had become a prestigious competition: Perlis, Kedah, Penang, Perak, Selangor, Negri Sembilan, Malacca, Johor, Kelantan, Terengganu, Pahang, Singapore, Malaysian Armed Forces, Singapore Joint

Services and the Commonwealth Forces. The format had been expanded to include military such as the Malaysian Armed Forces, Singapore Joint Services and the Commonwealth Forces teams.

In 1967, the HMS Malaya Cup was retired and replaced with a new trophy, the Piala Malaysia (Malaysia Cup), in line with political developments. Since then, the competition has been known as the Malaysia Cup. The old Malaya Cup now resides at the National Museum in Kuala Lumpur.

To everyone's surprise, Singapore withdrew from the Malaysia Cup in 1968. (They were to withdraw on two further occasions; once in 1982 and again in 1995, having rejoined in 1970 and 1985, respectively.) The withdrawal in 1968 came as a great shock for fans of the competition in Singapore and Malaysia. It represented a break in the 'oldest sports link' between the island and the mainland.

It was the Singapore government that took the decision to withdraw in 1968 rather than the FAS. In a letter to the FAS, then Minister for Social Affairs Othman Wok wrote that Singapore's continued participation in the Malaysia Cup was not in accordance with the nation's status as an independent republic. He also stated that the competition was a domestic competition between Malaysian states rather than a sports competition between sovereign nations.

While the Singapore government recognised the value of sport in building a national identity, it was not willing to tolerate any notion that newly independent Singapore was subordinate to Malaysia in any sphere, and this included sport.

The effect of Singapore's withdrawal from the Malaysia Cup in 1968 had disastrous consequences for the state of football in both nations. Singapore had always been one of the powerhouses of Malaysia Cup football since its inception in 1921. It had played in every final before the Second World War, and won the cup a total of 21 times.

By 1969, the Malaysia Cup lost more of its shine as the only other Singapore team, Singapore Joint Services, also withdrew from the competition.

The financial fallout was considerable as attendances at matches declined, and most states began the 1969 season in debt. Perak's deficit was $8,400 while Malacca was $7,000 in the red. The FAS suffered similar financial losses. Even prior to the withdrawal in 1968, the FAS had been in serious financial trouble. It was so poor that it was said that it could 'barely afford a six-cent stamp'.

Government support for the FAS was understandably weak, given other priorities in the incipient nation-state. The then Prime Minister of Singapore, Lee Kuan Yew, had once said, *"there are no national benefits from gold medallists from smaller countries.... and that it was foolish and wasteful for smaller countries to do it."* From 1966 to 1967, the FAS was technically bankrupt and even owed the government money.

The FAS was keen to get back into the Malaysia Cup competition and a golden opportunity was provided by an FAM invitation in 1969. Under the terms of a negotiated settlement between the FAM and the Singapore government, it would field a team from Singapore rather than a Singapore national team. The positional identity of the Singapore nation-state playing within a Malaysia framework in the post-independence period would be temporarily resolved by this distinction, which in truth only mattered to the politicians.

As far as the fans were concerned, they could once again resume their battle cries for Singapore against Malaysia.

While the earlier editions had been segmented into geographical zones (north and south), the 1979 edition saw a new format with every team playing each other in a 17-team competition. New entries were Federal Territory (later renamed Kuala Lumpur), the East Malaysian states of Sabah and Sarawak, as well as the independent sultanate of Brunei.

The top four teams in this new one-round league competition faced off in two semi-finals before the winners of each made it to the finals. In 1981, the quarter-final stage was introduced. When the league began, it was intended primarily as a qualifying tournament for the Piala Malaysia.

However, in 1982, the league trophy was awarded to the winners of the league stage. Since then, the Piala Malaysia has been held after the conclusion of the league each year, with only the best-performing teams in the league qualifying for the Piala Malaysia.

After Singapore's defeat against Selangor in the 1981 final, allegations of match-fixing and the involvement of bookies led to a three-week investigation by the Corrupt Practices Investigation Bureau. The probe, however, did not find evidence that Singapore players had accepted bribes.

In spite of the lack of evidence of any match-fixing, the FAM announced in November 1981 that Singapore would be excluded from the following year's Malaysia Cup. The expulsion was the result of two factors: crowd trouble during the semi-final match between Singapore and Johor in 1981, and the Malaysian state's threat to withdraw from the competition if Singapore remained in it.

Singapore returned to the tournament in 1985 and next won the Malaysia Cup in 1994. It exited the competition again the following year, after the FAM announced its intention to raise the levy on gate collections.

In addition, many in Singapore had also been calling for the country to set up its own professional league. In February 1995, then Football Association of Singapore President Ibrahim Othman announced Singapore's withdrawal from the Malaysia Cup, and the Singapore Professional Football League (S.League) was launched in 1996.

Another reason for Singapore's withdrawal from the Malaysia Cup in 1995 was the issue of match-fixing (again). The Malaysian police said that Singapore footballers were involved in match-fixing and bribery.

Following corruption charges against a player and a referee in Singapore in August 1994, the Malaysian police conducted match-fixing investigations into the Malaysian teams.

Eventually, more than 80 players faced punishment ranging from ban on playing for varying lengths of time to internal exile.

In 2000, club teams were allowed into the Malaysia Cup, which had previously been competed for only by state and military teams. In 2003, Selangor MPPJ became the first club to win the trophy.

In July 2011, the FAS announced that a Singapore team would participate in the Malaysia Cup as well as the Super League from 2012.

In 2015, the Football Malaysia Limited Liability Partnership was set up to privatise the Malaysian football league system. The partnership oversees five entities in Malaysian football, including the Malaysia Cup.

In November 2015, the FAM announced that it would not renew the partnership with the FAS, once again marking Singapore's exit from the Malaysian football scene.

While the Malaysia Cup would have provided Seng Quee with his most memorable achievement, his sights were always set beyond the Malaysia Cup. While Singapore's participation in the Malaysia Cup created a feverish atmosphere among football fans in Singapore,

Seng Quee always looked beyond this competition and was more concerned about Singapore's standing on the Asian stage.

In an interview with *The Straits Times* in June 1978, he had this to say about the Malaysia Cup:

> *"(The Malaysia Cup) to me, this is a small domestic tournament, made available to Singapore by special invitation from the Football Association of Malaysia. All participating teams are merely state teams within Malaysia, with the exception of Singapore — the only national team. If we cannot win the Malaysia Cup, we may as well pack up!*
>
> *"We have to be realistic in whatever we do in soccer. I said this a long time ago. I will say it again and again.*
>
> *"Let me be blunt: We cannot improve our standard by competing in the Malaysia Cup year in and year out, even for another 100 years. We cannot gauge our standard by taking the Malaysia Cup results as a yardstick. Our goal should be the very pinnacle of Asian soccer."*

Hence, it is ironic that it was as a player representing Singapore in the Malaya Cup (as it was known until 1967) that Seng Quee made his mark as a talented defender. He was part of the Singapore team that won the Malaya Cup in 1937 and 1939.

But more of that later as we now look back into the formative years of Seng Quee.

Chapter Three

Family Life

Tuesday, 1 December 1914: The clouds of war hovered around Europe. On that day, the King of England, George V, paid a visit to the headquarters of the British army in Paris. Five months earlier, on 28 June 1914, Archduke Franz Ferdinand, heir to the Austrian throne, and his wife were shot and killed by a lone assassin while visiting Sarajevo in Bosnia. That assassination sparked a series of events which eventually culminated in the First World War.

On that same day (1 December 1914), the silent film, Broncho Billy, was being screened at the Alhambra cinema in Beach Road. The Alhambra cinema, with a capacity of almost 3,500, was one of the largest cinemas in Singapore during that period. The cinema was situated right next to the beach along Beach Road which led to the locals calling the cinema by its Hokkien name 'hai kee', which translates to 'by the sea'.

In the Wearne Brothers car showroom in Orchard Road, the Studebaker Four was on sale for a princely sum of $2,400.

Meanwhile, a short article in *The Straits Times* spoke about Mr. C. de St. Céran of Moine Compte and Co. who was the first Singaporean to leave for the European Front on 4 August 1914. He expressed his jubilation upon receiving a copy of *The Straits Times* while at the Front.

While all these local and international events took place, Koh Yew Kum bore a son whom she called Joseph Choo Seng Quee (Chinese: 朱成贵; pinyin: Zhū Chéngguì;). Though it was not the news of the day, the larger-than-life person bearing the name 'Choo Seng Quee' would feature regularly in the sporting pages of the major newspapers in Singapore, Malaysia and Indonesia for almost half a century until his death in 1983. (Note: Chinese names come with the surname first followed by a personal name. 'Choo' was Seng Quee's surname while his personal name was 'Seng Quee'. In this book, I have mainly referred to him by his personal name and in some cases as 'Uncle Choo' as he was affectionately known as by many people.)

It was rather fortunate that the First World War did not affect Singapore adversely. This allowed Seng Quee to grow up in relatively peaceful settings. The only significant event that took place in Singapore during this time was the 1915 Singapore Mutiny (also known as the 1915 Sepoy Mutiny or the Mutiny of the 5th Light Infantry). The Singapore Mutiny involved almost 800 sepoys (Indian soldiers) and resulted in the deaths of almost 30 people (including eight British officers, two Malay officers, one soldier and 14 British civilians).

Seng Quee's family came from Bangka Belitung islands off the south eastern coasts of Sumatra. Bangka Belitung has a long history with Chinese migration (mainly Hakka people which Choo Seng Quee's family was part of). Chinese people in the 13th century had already started to migrate into the Bangka region. The Hakkas in Bangka Belitung originated from Southern China, especially the Guangdong province, migrating from the 18th century to the early 20th century to have better job opportunities. The word 'Hakka' literally means 'guest families'.

In the 17th century, the rulers of Palembang saw extraordinary potential in Belitung when they found tin mines on the island. The name 'Bangka' is derived from the word '*wangka*' meaning 'tin' in Sanskrit, because this region is indeed rich in tin mining. The tin is the primary reason why the Dutch decided to bring contract workers from mainland China and resettle them in Belitung. Tin mining is a tough industry. The people from the islands had a tough work ethic.

For Seng Quee, that work ethic instilled in him by his forefathers is very much part of the character of the people from Bangka Belitung: saving the soul through industry, effort, honest labour and giving one's all to the job. It may also be coincidental that many great managers from the UK like Sir Matt Busby, Bill Shankly and Sir Alex Ferguson (all Scotsmen), had origins from mining towns.

According to N. Ganesan, former Chairman of the Football Association of Singapore, the Bangka Belitung islands had a legacy for producing great footballers. In addition to Seng Quee, there were also Kee Yew Leng and Ha Tee Siang and many of the players of the Straits Chinese Football Association before the Second World War, originated from these islands.

In fact, before the Second World War, there was a Banka Sports Club which was formed in 1937 and which featured players who originated from the Bangka Belitung islands. Seng Quee was the secretary of the club.

Seng Quee lived with his parents and four brothers (Seng Kay, Seng Choon, Seng Hock and Seng Chye) at 212R Rangoon Road.

According to a newspaper report from 1949, during Seng Quee's teenage days during the late 1920s, it was music that dominated the Choo household. Music, especially Western classical music, was considered a pursuit of the rich and educated.

A teenage Seng Quee was handed a violin to fill the air at home with the vibrations of Beethoven and Mozart. By the age of 16, he was taking regular music lessons. But football was always his passion and he started skipping his violin classes.

According to that same newspaper report from 1949, his brother was so enraged that he skipped his violin classes for football that he destroyed Seng Quee's jersey and boots. He only relented several years later when Seng Quee was chosen to represent Singapore in the Malaya Cup and made amends by buying Seng Quee a set of football equipment.

Seng Quee's teenage years were spent in a Singapore experiencing the same roller-coaster effect that Western economies did in the period between the two world wars. A post-war boom created by rising tin and rubber prices gave way to recession in the late 1920s when prices for both dropped on the world market.

In his 1934 book, *The Lights of Singapore*, Sir Roland Braddell described Singapore in the early 1930s as follows:

> *"When you come into Singapore the whole place seems so new, so very George the Fifth. Up overhead seaplanes circle; opposite the wharves is a brand-new railway station; you roll into town along a road both sides of which implore you not to be vague but to order Haig, or try somebody's silk stockings or somebody else's cigarettes; the streets are full of motor traffic; most of the big buildings which you pass seem quite new; and, if you are English, you get an impression of a kind of tropical cross between Manchester and Liverpool."*

And it was in the 1930s when Seng Quee made his grand entry into the football world as a player.

Chapter Four

Seng Quee: The Player

Like many other kids growing up in Singapore in the 1920s and 1930s, Seng Quee would have most probably kicked his first football with some other enthusiastic kids on the many fields doting the island (though it has been reported that he learnt his football while studying for his Senior Cambridge certificate at Raffles Institution). These boys would have imagined themselves being the stars of that day, like Dolfattah, John Then or Mat Noor.

Playing football on the streets was an uncomplicated affair for these boys. Two teams (sometimes as many as 20 players on each side) would use sticks or slippers to form makeshift goal posts. Inelegant but effective. It did its job in marking the goal of the teams — to score more than the other. Games could last for hours until the sun went down or when the kids finally heeded to the shouts from their parents in the nearby houses. It would have been here that Seng Quee picked up the fundamentals of ball control.

Those street football skills would have come in handy when Seng Quee started his formal football training at Raffles Institution.

Raffles Institution (or 'RI' as it is more affectionately known to many Singaporeans) was one of Singapore's first-ever schools. It was founded by Sir Stamford Raffles in 1823 and was originally known as the Singapore Institution.

Seng Quee's first game for the Raffles School XI was in the inter-school competition of 1930. He played at right full-back and was probably one of the fortunate ones who had a pair of football boots.

Football boots were a luxury in those days and even up to the 1960s, many boys could not afford a pair of boots. Many future players would not forget the generosity Seng Quee demonstrated when, as owner of Maju Jaya Sports Store in the 1960s, he gave free boots to players who could not afford a pair. But, more on that later.

Seng Quee was fortunate to have football legend, 'Pop' Lim Yong Liang, as a mentor. 'Pop' was considered by many to be the greatest inside-forward that Singapore has ever produced. Seng Quee said that 'Pop' discovered him playing in the old Raffles Institution field in Bras Basah Road and was impressed by his ability.

Other sources mention the possibility that 'Pop' knew someone in Raffles Institution and had seen Seng Quee play by chance during one of his visits there.

Whatever the case may have been, that chance meeting and 'Pop's continued guidance of Seng Quee proved to be a vital factor in enhancing Seng Quee's progress in football. But who exactly was 'Pop' Lim?

'Pop' Lim Yong Liang

Theo Leijssius (a former Singapore international) proclaimed him as "the greatest centre forward I had ever seen", in an interview in 1975.

For many, he is referred to as the 'Grand Old Man of Singapore Soccer'. For some who were fortunate enough to witness his magical skills in the flesh, they portray him as having the slick skills of '70s star Mohamed Noh, the power of accuracy of Malaysian striker Mokhtar Dahari and the dash of Quah Kim Song!

'Pop' Lim Yong Liang was a Singapore football legend and a household name in the 1920s and 1930s. Except for the Japanese Occupation of Singapore from 1942 to 1945, 'Pop' was closely connected with Singapore football throughout his life. He appeared in every Malaya Cup final that Singapore contested in from 1922 to 1928 (except the 1924 final).

He started out with the Straits Chinese Football Association (SCFA)team in 1915 when he was only 15 years old. His impressive performances led to his debut in representative football in 1919 donning the colours of White Star FC, one of the leading clubs during that post-war generation. By 1922, he had proven to everyone that he was good enough to represent Singapore. He was selected for the 1922 Malaya Cup. Singapore made it to the final that year and though 'Pop' scored in his debut final in Kuala Lumpur, Singapore did not return home with the Malaya Cup.

He was a regular in the Singapore team until 1928. Altogether he played in a record six Malaya Cup finals and was on the winning side only once. He bagged a total of three goals in those finals.

In 1934, he was recalled to the Singapore side to play in a Malaya Cup match against Malacca which Singapore won. (Such was his value to the team that he would be recalled once more seven years later at the ripe old age of 41!). His philosophy of constant practice, keeping regular hours and having moderation in everything ensured his longevity in football. His belief in constant practice was transmitted to Seng Quee who drilled this home to future players like Rahim Omar and later to R. Suria Murthi.

And when it was time to hang up those mercurial boots, he became a referee and a coach. He coached SCFA from 1933 to 1940.

His growing reputation as a formidable coach did not escape the eyes of the Singapore Amateur Football Association (SAFA). From

1937 to 1941, he was assigned as the official coach of the Singapore team. Under his stewardship, Singapore won the Malaya Cup in 1937, 1939, 1940 and 1941.

His commitment to the Singapore cause continued after the end of the Second World War. He was appointed as secretary of SAFA, a post he would hold for more than 20 years, though he did on more than one occasion try to step down but was persuaded to continue on.

His contributions did not go unnoticed. He was decorated with the MBE (Member of the Order of the British Empire) in 1959 and the BBM (Bintang Bakti Masyarakat [Public Service Star]) in 1964 for services rendered to sports. In 1966, he was appointed life Vice-President of the Football Association of Singapore (FAS). But he was back in the secretary's chair from 1968–1971. He was also a football advisor to the National Sports Promotion Board (1972) and FAS (1973).

And when 'Pop' celebrated his 80th birthday in 1980, among the congratulatory telegrams he received was one from an old friend in England, Sir Matt Busby, a legendary coach of Manchester United who was best known for leading the English team to win the European Cup in 1968.

So it was under the wings of 'Pop' Lim that Seng Quee had his first involvement with club football in 1933. Seng Quee was only 19 years old. The team that gave him his start was the SCFA.

Straits Chinese Football Association

The Straits Chinese Football Association (SCFA) was the first local or Asian team to break the dominance of the European teams in Singapore by winning the Singapore league in 1925. They were league champions again in 1930, 1934, 1937, and 1938.

Established in Singapore in 1911, it was initially set up to promote football amongst the Chinese community in colonial Singapore. The Chinese had been excluded from competitive football organised by the then recently created Malay Football Association (MFA) (formed in 1909), hence the need to create their own association.

The founding President of the SCFA was Dr. Yin Suat Chuan. He was a Member of the Singapore Municipal Council (1912) and Director of the Chinese Commercial Bank Limited (1912–1913). He was also the first Chinese doctor to practise in Singapore. (His family had their own interesting history; his son, Leslie Charteris [born Leslie Charles Bowyer-Yin] was best known for his many books chronicling the adventures of the charming anti-hero Simon Templar, alias 'The Saint.' His sister, Grace Yin Peck Ha, was the second wife of Dr. Lim Boon Keng, a Peranakan physician who promoted social and educational reforms in Singapore in the early 20th-century and now has a Mass Rapid Transit station and two roads in Singapore named after him.)

From its initiation, the SCFA only accepted Chinese players for its teams. It organised its first cup competition for Chinese teams in 1911. Known as the Fairy Dale Cup, it attracted eight clubs: White Star Club I, White Star Club II, Mount Wallich Club, Juvenile Football Club I, Mercantile Bank Football Club II, Bukit Bahru Football Club I, Bukit Bahru Football Club II, and St. Joseph's Institution.

The Association eventually changed its name from Straits Chinese Football Association to Singapore Chinese Football Association in 1945.

Seng Quee's debut

According to some historians, the decade from 1930 to 1940 was considered as the watermark of Singapore football. This was a period that saw Singapore continuing to enter the Malaya Cup final every year before the war and produced some of the greatest players in cup annals.

Organised football was also on the rise. By the 1930s, there were three divisions in the SAFA league. The growing interest in the game meant that more football clubs were created. The SAFA league had been extended to two divisions in 1921. By 1930, there was a need for a further division and a reserve division was created which later became known as the third division.

It was here in the third tier that Seng Quee made his league debut in 1933. He was still a student in Raffles Institution then and was playing for the RI team. The RI team played a friendly match with the SCFA third team on 3 March 1933 and Seng Quee's performance convinced SCFA that he could be a right fit for the team. (Though he started playing for SCFA, he did continue to play for RI until he completed his studies at the end of 1933.) That would have meant that his days were filled with studies during the day and training sessions in the evenings.

Seng Quee started off as a right full-back in SCFA's third team. The SCFA had one team in each of the three divisions. Those 'green' and 'wet behind the ears' players started out in the third team and Seng Quee was no exception. Their progress to the senior teams depended on their performances on the field. For Seng Quee, that progress was rapid. His colossal figure must have terrorised opponents. His six-foot (1.82-metre) frame towered over most opponents. His defensive partner was Tan Kong Guan who later became the ground superintendent. (In those days, teams played with only two defenders in a 2-3-5 formation.) This defensive partnership played a pivotal role in the SCFA third team that year as they swept away with the third division title winning all their games and only conceding eight goals in 14 matches.

The impressive displays carried on the following year when Seng Quee was elevated to the SCFA second team. The 1934 season proved to be a successful one too as Seng Quee and his teammates overcame all opposition to win the league. 'Pop' Lim who had come out of retirement was also in the SCFA second team. It must have been a thrill for Seng Quee to be in the same team as his former mentor.

That year also saw Seng Quee represent Government Monopolies in the Government Services league. And he also had time to play for his alma mater, Raffles Institution Old Boys, whenever his services were required.

Of course, for all players back then, football was played at amateur level. Most players had a daytime job. And Seng Quee was no different. Fresh faced and just out of school, Seng Quee found employment at the Malayan Establishment Office (MEO) (which later became the Public Services Department). The task of the MEO was to recruit civil servants (both local and British) for the civil service. Seng Quee was in the Medical department of the MEO.

Any spare time that Seng Quee had was devoted to football. With the blessing given by his family who realised there was sporting talent in the family (his brother, Choo Seng Kay, was an accomplished water polo player), Seng Quee took every opportunity to immerse himself in the game.

Seng Quee's football education continued and his progress was rapid. In 1935 at the tender age of 21, he was promoted to the first team where he played alongside Kee Yew Leng, his team mate and captain from his Raffles Institution school days. Success came almost immediately when the SCFA team finished runner-up in the league competition. They did triumph in the SAFA Challenge Cup, though surprisingly, Seng Quee did not feature in the final. The glory for that final belonged to Quan Chong, who spearheaded the attack in the SCFA team masterminded by their captain, John Then. Quan Chong bagged three goals in their 3-1 victory against an MFA team weakened by the absence of their star striker, Mat Noor. Mat had the misfortune of injuring his knee during their semi-final clash against a rather physical Royal Engineers team.

By now, Seng Quee was a player in demand. His services were sought after by many teams playing in other league or cup competitions in Singapore. Many of the league and cup competitions only lasted a few months in a year. This meant that clubs could obtain his services when one competition was over. For football-mad Seng Quee, this meant that he could play football throughout the year.

By 1936, in addition to his appearances for SCFA, he also wore the colours of the Mercantile Institute as well as Singapore Rovers who did a tour of Malacca. Added to that, he was also active in the Chinese league representing Aston Athletic Club. He even played in friendlies for a team called United Mackenzie Footers! As part of the MEO, Seng Quee also represented the Government Services football team in several matches in 1936 and 1937.

Debut in the national team

Like all the players during that era, Seng Quee was constantly eyeing the topmost rung of Singapore football. He, together with many other SCFA players, wanted a place in the prestigious Malaya Cup team. But competition for the team was keen. Waiting on the wings were many other talented players. Often, the selectors had a difficult time determining the line-up.

But Seng Quee worked hard and his impressive performances for SCFA in the SAFA league were finally rewarded when it was announced in the newspapers on 4 May 1936 that the muscular six-footer had been selected to attend a trial to select the team to represent Singapore in the Malaya Cup. Thirty-one players had been shortlisted. The list included many of the stars of the day like his teammates, John Then, Quan Chong and Chia Keng Hock as well as established players like A.G. Valberg, Said bin Sidik and Dollah. To his joy, Seng Quee found his name as one of the 16 players selected to represent Singapore in the Malaya Cup.

The year 1936 was significant in many ways. Berlin had been awarded the 1936 Olympic Games. Adolf Hitler, the German Chancellor, took the opportunity to launch his masterful propaganda campaign to promote his Nazi party. Led by his propaganda chief, Joseph Goebbels, the Nazis used the games to expound their manifesto of the superiority of the 'Aryan' race. Thankfully, their efforts were thwarted in a huge way by an African American, Jesse Owens. Owens embarrassed the Führer and took home four gold medals in the track and field competition. That angered Hitler so much that he refused to attend the medal award ceremony whenever Owens stood on the medal podium.

But for many countries, Nazi propaganda was the least of their worries. The Chinese football team, who were participating in the Games for the first time, played a series of warm-up matches to get themselves ready for the competition. (They eventually lost to Great Britain in their first round fixture and were eliminated from the tournament.) Interestingly, three Singaporeans were selected to represent China at the Games: Chua Boon Lay, Tay Quee Liang and Chee Ah Hui.

One of their warm-up matches was against Singapore. Seng Quee was selected to represent the Singapore team in that friendly. A record crowd of 25,000 spectators witnessed that game which was played at the Anson Road Stadium. The Chinese team easily won that game by four goals to nil. But for Seng Quee, it was a dream come true to play against the Chinese forward, Lee Wai Tong.

Who was Lee Wai Tong? According to N. Ganesan, former Chairman of FAS, Lee Wai Tong was Seng Quee's hero. He is often regarded as the greatest Chinese footballer due to his accomplishments in winning several Far Eastern Games titles with the national team. He also led the Chinese national football squad to their first-ever Olympic tournament in 1936. This was also followed by having an extremely successful club career with South China where he won eight league titles with them, helping to establish the club as the most successful team in Hong Kong history at the time. After his retirement, he moved into management where he guided the Republic of China to victory in the 1954 Asian Games.

For the Singapore team in 1936, the Olympic Games was not within their radar. Their barometer of success was the Malaya Cup. Winning the cup was the main objective of the Singapore selectors. Finishing second was not an option. But it was Selangor who emerged as the top dogs for the 1936 season. With a finely balanced team led by A. L. Henry, the Selangor team swept past their opponents with ease and edged the Singapore team by one goal to nil in the final at the Anson Road Stadium. Though Seng Quee featured in many of the qualifying games, he did not make it to the team for the final. But his grand opportunity was to come in the following year.

The year 1937 proved to be a successful one for the young midfielder, both at club and at national level. Seng Quee was now part of the half-line (now known as midfield) in the SCFA team. Together with Kee Yew Leng and Koh Hor Khoon, they were acknowledged as the best half-line in the peninsula (Singapore and Malaya). This near impregnable defence wall had a legendary reputation for snuffing out any attacking initiatives from the opposing side. It came as no surprise that SCFA clinched the 'double' by winning both the SAFA Senior League and the SAFA Challenge Cup.

This magnificent trio also formed the backbone of the Singapore team. They played a vital role in helping the Singapore team win the Malaya Cup in 1937 when they beat arch-rivals Selangor 2-1 at the Selangor Club Padang in Kuala Lumpur.

It was a fact that selectors tried to keep the line intact. On a number of occasions when the line was broken (usually due to circumstances beyond the officials' control), disaster came upon the team and this was immediately followed by a public outcry as to why so and so of the trio was left out.

But the trio could not save Singapore from defeat the following year when Selangor exacted revenge from their loss a year earlier.

As a player, Choo Seng Quee was the classic centre-half of his generation; aggressive, punishing but always honest. Standing at 6 feet with his slicked back hair, he was a terrifying prospect for any opponent. He excelled as a leader on the field, motivating his fellow players to urge them on. It was hardly surprising that even before he retired as a player, he had already landed himself a coaching job in 1939.

Seng Quee also featured in several matches for the Sino-Malays team. The Sino-Malays team was made up of the cream of players from the SCFA and the MFA. They were not a team in the real sense of the word. They were only brought together whenever there was a need for a strong local side to play against a foreign team. In an interview given in 1975, Mat Noor, Singapore's greatest inside-forward, said that the Sino-Malays team never trained together. On the day of the game, the players selected from each association would turn up on the field and meet each other for the first time! That fact made their most sensational victory against a highly fancied Australian team in 1928 even more exceptional!

Seng Quee donned the Sino-Malays colours for a few matches. His last match for them was a charity game against the Combined Forces a few months before the Japanese Occupation of Singapore. The match was in aid of the China Relief Fund, the Malaya Patriotic Fund and the War Fund. Sino-Malays won the match 2-0.

Apart from the Malaya Cup, Seng Quee was also in the Singapore team that participated in several international matches towards the tail end of the 1930s.

In 1937, the Singapore team hopped on board the cargo ship, 'Gouvernuer General Pasquier' destined for Saigon to play several international matches in the Vietnamese capital. The team was made up of the following players: Flight Lieut. Messenger (captain), Gunner. Pipe, Gunner. Buckley, Private Croy, L.A.C. Northgrave, Choo Seng Quee, Koh Hor Khoon, Kee Yew Leng, Soon Choon Lye, C. D. Kronenberg, Sarip Abdul Rahman, Said, Taib and Dollah.

Their first game was against Saigon Union. It was played under floodlights, a novelty for the Singapore team. The game ended in a 1-1 draw. According to a Saigon newspaper report, the heavy downpour deterred many from witnessing an excellent game. The Singapore team was not used to having a match at a later than usual time. Hence, many of them actually had dinner before the game which, not surprisingly affected some players including Kee Yew Leng who had to leave the field at half-time due to a bout of colic.

Their second game against a French team finished in a 1-0 victory. However, it was reported that coach Lim Yong Liang was unhappy with the erratic performance of the team.

The Singapore team saved the best for the last providing a scintillating display to overcome a resilient Saigon team by three goals to one.

At the end of the tour, Seng Quee was voted as one of the best halves ever to have visited Saigon.

His excellent performances, both with SCFA and the Singapore team resulted in him being selected for several tours with the Singapore team to Saigon, Hong Kong and Macau.

Seng Quee's greatest trait as a player seems to have been his vision and strength.

The Sunday Tribune provided a profile of all the Singapore Chinese players (which included Seng Quee) who were selected to go on a Far East tour in 1939. This is how he was profiled:

Choo Seng Quee (Centre-half)

Age 25: Singapore's centre-half. A tall and impressive figure in such a vital position who closes very ably the gap down the middle. Usually takes penalties for the side and got many goals from the corner kicks awarded to his side by his headwork. Rather temperamental. Has played in Java, Shanghai and Saigon. Seems to play better as a defensive centre-half than an attacking one. Malaya Cup representative 1937 and 1938.

Their Far East tour to Manila, Hong Kong and Saigon was significant in that they were reputedly the first Asian football side to travel by air. Air travel in the 1930s was a glamorous affair for the privileged, the rich and the famous. So it must have been a huge thrill for Seng Quee and his teammates to travel by air.

His impressive performances during the Far East tour caught the attention of the Chinese selectors. He was invited to attend the preliminary selection in Hong Kong. The Chinese team was made up of Chinese players from the Singapore and Hong Kong teams. He impressed the Chinese selectors so much that he was mentioned as a certain choice and was to be part of the 15-man Chinese football team that was to take part in the 1940 Olympics in Tokyo (which was subsequently moved to Helsinki).

For many Chinese players in Singapore, the opportunity to play for China was a great 'feather in their cap' and for Seng Quee, it was no different. Sadly, the declaration of war in Europe forced the cancellation of the 1940 Olympic Games and with it went Seng Quee's dreams of playing on a larger stage.

It must have been heart-breaking for Seng Quee. He was only 26 years old and was at the peak of his career. Reading through the editions of *The Straits Times* and other local newspapers from the 1930s, it was clear that Seng Quee was a bright prospect in Singapore football.

Seng Quee's career continued at club level. By now, he had formed a team, Chinese Athletic, and took the role of player-coach, which would be his first coaching stint.

The Japanese Occupation of Singapore put an end to all sporting activities. For Seng Quee, the war would put a sad end to the promising career of a great footballer. It is impossible to know what he might have achieved and how different the annals of the game might look, had the war not intervened.

Chapter Five

The War Years

T he Second World War most definitely stunted the development of many players in Singapore. For Seng Quee, it must have been devastating since the war stole some of his peak years.

War in Singapore began on 8 December 1941, when Japanese planes dropped the first bombs on the island, killing 61 and injuring 133 people. Sensing the nation's vulnerability and lack of defence preparations by the British, Japanese troops began their invasion from the north in Malaya and eventually reached the shores of Singapore on 8 February 1942. This day marked the start of the Battle for Singapore, which ended on 15 February 1942 — the day the British officially surrendered Singapore to the Japanese.

The Japanese Occupation in Singapore lasted for three anguishing years. After numerous defeats, including the atomic bombing of Hiroshima on 6 August 1945, the Japanese officially surrendered on 2 September 1945, ending the Second World War.

To piece together what happened to Seng Quee during the Second World War, we have to rely principally on several newspaper sources as precious little detail of this time in his life survives. We know that in 1941, Seng Quee played for the Sing Tao club in Hong Kong and that during the Pacific War he was in Macau, and later, Free China. The *Singapore Standard* reported on a magistrates hearing in 1954 where Seng Quee revealed to the court that he was a secret spy agent for the British during the Japanese Occupation. (He confirmed this during an interview with Joe Dorai, a journalist from *The Straits Times*, in 1978.)

He also added to Joe Dorai that he was the manager of *The Macao Tribune* (*Aomen Luntanbao*) which was sponsored by the British. He wrote propaganda for the British without getting caught. He also proudly claimed that he smuggled the fiancée of a Singapore friend from Macau to China.

"*My absence became known to the Japanese and I had to walk back from China to Macau. It took me five nights*", he added. Despite his activities, he was never caught during the Japanese Occupation. Whether some of these facts were true or not, we can never tell.

For those players who persevered with football during the Japanese Occupation in Singapore, the opportunities to continue with their passion were few and far in between. There were other more pressing concerns. Singapore faced a severe food shortage. In a 1975 interview with Gan Kee Siang, a former Singapore footballer, he recalled an incident during the war where the players were told that they would be having a training session. When they arrived at the Padang, they were instead handed 'changkuls' (a type of hoe) and forced to grow tapioca roots on their beloved training ground!

Kee Siang who played with Seng Quee in the Singapore Cup winning side of 1937, did acknowledge that there were some perks given to the players for their football services, like going on two goodwill missions to Malaya as part of a Japanese-organised team called Syonan-Tu. In addition, players were given rice and cigarettes as incentives while most people had to subsist on sweet potatoes and tapioca only.

Another great Singapore footballer from the 1940s and 1950s, Ivan Vass recalled one of their tours to Malaya. Before leaving for the tour, one of the senior Japanese officers offered a strange warning to the players. *"You can lose to any town in Malaya except Kuala Lumpur"*! It was only later that the players found out that the officer had placed a huge bet on the outcome of the match against KL. Had they lost, the officer would have lost quite a bit of money. (Fortunately, the Singapore team won 4-2 and the players were spared from any unpleasant repercussions.)

Following the Japanese surrender in 1945, it took a while before a semblance of normality resumed in Singapore. Food and medical supplies were dangerously low, partly because shipping was in total disarray. Allied bombing had taken its toll on Singapore's harbour facilities, and numerous wrecks blocked the harbour. Electricity, gas, water, and telephone services were in serious disrepair. Severe overcrowding had resulted in thousands of squatters living in shanties, and the death rate was twice the pre-war level.

It is unclear whether Seng Quee returned to Singapore in 1945 or 1946 but he did resume his role as player-coach of Chinese Athletic in 1946. That marked the beginning of a coaching legacy that would spread over a period of almost 40 years.

Chapter Six

Seng Quee: The Coach

Choo Seng Quee's coaching career actually commenced just before the war. In 1939, he surprised everyone by leaving the Straits Chinese Football Association (SCFA). He had been a regular stalwart for almost six years. He had helped turn them into a force to be reckoned with. Few people know the actual reasons why he left. Soon after he departed, he founded a new club called Chinese Athletic (or C.A. as they were more popularly known as). Here, he performed the dual role of player and coach. Thus began his venture into the world of coaching at the youthful age of 25.

Most footballers in Singapore and in fact those countries where football was played at an amateur level, would only have a career that spans a period of 10 to 15 years. Anything beyond that is considered as a bonus. Many of them went back to their day jobs once they retired. For those aspiring to remain in the game after their playing days are over, the next logical step would be to become a coach. That way, they could remain in the game as well as impart all the valuable knowledge and experience that they have acquired to the next generation of players.

Today, it has become the norm for every national team coach in Asia to have the AFC (Asian Football Confederation) Professional Coaching Diploma. (The AFC considers the diploma to be the equivalent of the UEFA Pro-Licence qualification.) Those who strive to acquire this diploma need to first complete the 'A' coaching certificate. Studying for the diploma involves undertaking at least 220 hours of coursework. The course would cover all sorts of areas from psychology and media management to tactics and sports science. It is a long process and even then, once you have passed, there are few guarantees.

Like most other coaches in the 1940s and 1950s, Seng Quee descended onto the coaching world without any such certificates. He, like the others, had only to depend on their past experience as a player or through constant observation of the game.

For Seng Quee, this ability to coach came almost naturally. Apart from a six-month coaching bursary in the UK in 1961, everything else was self-taught. N. Ganesan, former Football Association of Singapore (FAS) Chairman, recollected that Seng Quee always kept a book with scribblings and drawings related to football. *"He was always keeping himself up-to-date with the latest developments in football"*, Ganesan said. In a newspaper interview given in 1975, Seng Quee even quipped that he once took notes while watching a screening of a World Cup match in a cinema in Chinatown during the 1950s!

Influences

Who would have Seng Quee been influenced by, as a coach? We can only speculate that Seng Quee's decision to start coaching was heavily influenced by 'Pop' Lim Yong Liang. As mentioned earlier, 'Pop' was the person who discovered Seng Quee and trained him when he was in Singapore's Malaya Cup squad in 1937.

But being the person who was constantly in search of new and better ideas, it is plausible that he was also influenced by the great coaches of the 1930s.

The 1930s saw the rise of Arsenal Football Club. They were coached by the mythical Herbert Chapman. Chapman had made his name in the 1920s leading Huddersfield Town, a modest football club from the Yorkshire area in England, to successive English titles. By the time they were on their way to the treble of league titles, Chapman had already been prized away by the ever-ambitious Arsenal.

It was Chapman who was credited with introducing the 'WM' system in 1926. This new development could have been precipitated by the change to the offside law in England a year earlier. The new offside law demanded that, for a forward player to be onside, only two opposing players (usually a goalkeeper and one defender) had to be between him and his opponent's goal. The old offside law which had been in force since 1866 required three opposing players between the forward and the opponent's goal to remain onside.

Chapman changed the traditional line-up of two full-backs, three half-backs and five forwards by making the centre-half a third central full-back (also to become known as the stopper) with the two full-backs pivoting around him. With the 'M' below the 'W' they formed the bottom three points of the 'M' and the top two points were the two wing-halves. The two bottom points of the 'W' were the inside-forwards and the top three points were the two wingers and the centre-forward. They did not use numbers to describe the formation in those days but if they did, the literal transposition of 'WM' might have been 3-4-3. The full-backs marked the wingers rather than inside-forwards, the wing-halves sat on the opposing inside-forwards rather than on the wingers, the centre-half, now a centre-back, dealt with the centre-forward, and both inside-forwards dropped deeper.

It was a revolutionary system which brought great success to the London clubs resulting in Arsenal dominating the English scene in the 1930s.

With his constant appetite of devouring new tactics and strategies, it will not be a surprise if Seng Quee picked up some of Chapman's strategies.

Seng Quee could also have been influenced by the great pioneer of Austrian football, Hugo Meisl. Meisl was instrumental in the rise of the Austrian 'Wunderteam' of the 1930s led by the brilliant Matthias Sindelar. He was a new style of centre-forward, a player of slight stature that he was nicknamed 'Der Papierene' — 'the Paper-man'.

Though the Austrian team played in the traditional 2-3-5 system, they blended it with an elegant attacking centre-half in Josef Smistik and an unorthodox centre-forward in Sindelaar who encouraged fluidity in the system. Sindelaar would play football as a grandmaster would play chess — with a broad mental conception, calculating moves and countermoves in advance, always choosing the most promising of all possibilities.

In an article written by Seng Quee in 1976, he referred to the idea of 'whirl football' (or 'total football') as was mooted by Dr. Willy Meisl. In whirl football, each player must be an all-rounder, equally adept in both defence and attack. However, Seng Quee knew that though whirl football was the ideal in football, it was probably too ideal in an era where football was dominated by safety-first tactics as was the case in the 1970s.

Full-time coach

Having already started performing the role of player-coach with Chinese Athletic in 1939, he eventually decided to concentrate solely on coaching in 1949. As he recollected to a journalist in 1949, his decision to retire from playing football was due to two reasons. Firstly, it was due to his increasing weight. (In his prime as a centre-half, Seng Quee weighed 146lb [66 kg] but by 1949, his weight had gone up to 207 lb [94 kg].) Secondly, it was his intention to devote all his spare time to coaching the younger players.

Seng Quee set upon to apply the methods that he had learned to his Chinese Athletic team but he always harboured the ambition to become the coach of the Singapore national team.

That opportunity came in March 1949 when he was selected to train the Singapore national team to prepare them for the 1949 Malaya Cup campaign. He was only 34 years old.

The officials at the Singapore Amateur Football Association (SAFA) were aware that Seng Quee had a sound knowledge of football and was wholeheartedly interested in the game. They also said that he was a staunch advocate of clean football which they felt was a good virtue for a coach to possess.

Back then, coaches in Singapore were hired on a competition by competition basis, that is, their tenure only lasted for the weeks or months prior to a tournament and ended when the competition was over.

Seng Quee had already prepared a strict training programme for this highly desired role. Training sessions were held on Tuesdays, Thursdays and Saturdays at the Jalan Besar Stadium.

The training sessions started at 6.30pm after league games. Most league games commenced at 5pm back then as there were no floodlights in the stadiums.

The 1949 season saw a record of 70 teams participating in the various SAFA leagues. Hence many of his players were involved in league games before starting their training.

The first 30 minutes of the training session was spent discussing tactics, physical culture and the finer points of the game. With his wealth of knowledge, it must have been interesting as well as bewildering for some of his players who came from families where education might not have been a priority.

Players had to undergo the following routine three times a week: running laps around the field, bodybuilding exercises, dribbling with the ball round sticks placed at various distances, passing in pairs, sprinting with the ball from a stationary position, standing still and going into action, hitting the ball straight ahead and chasing it as fast as possible, trapping and easy running with sudden bursts of speed, passing movements, kicking a dead ball and kicking a ball travelling in the same and opposite directions.

Forwards also had shooting practice from all angles, while goalkeepers were trained in the continental style — that is, a ball is thrown at a goalkeeper from a few feet away from all angles for a full 10 minutes.

There was a high turnout at each training session (80 percent attendance) which was considered high during that era considering that all the players were amateurs and most had regular daytime jobs. If there were any absentees at the training sessions, it was mainly due to league matches in which some of the players had to participate, though many still went for the training sessions after their league games.

Even back then, Seng Quee's approach was also characterised by an unprecedented attention to players' diet, and by an obsessive focus on the minutest detail — the condition of the pitch or the position of the sun — which might somehow present his team with a narrow advantage.

Strict discipline was enforced and Seng Quee had no qualms about dropping players who were absent from training sessions without any valid reason. He always highlighted the importance of keeping fit. For him, that was the only way to bring back the Malaya Cup to Singapore.

His Singapore team did well enough to make it to the semi-finals of the Malaya Cup. In the semi-finals, they met the newly formed Army-Navy team. Seng Quee was confident that his fighting fit team would be able to overcome the tough Army-Navy team. Sadly, that was not to be the case and they were defeated by the military men inspired by the brilliance of their twin attackers of J. G. Todd and Bert Inglis.

The semi-final defeat concluded Seng Quee's first coaching stint as coach of Singapore. It was a relatively short stint which, sadly, would mirror all his four other appointments as Singapore coach. Each appointment would last no more than two years and in one case, 10 days!

Like many coaches during that era, Seng Quee was allowed to perform dual roles, that is, coaching the Singapore national team as well as Chinese Athletic (and in Seng Quee's case, multiple roles). According to Justin Morais (who played for Tampines Rovers football club in the early 1950s and is well known in the Singapore football community for his work in alternative medical therapies like acupuncture and homeopathy), Seng Quee was also the combined schools coach in 1949.

In addition to those roles mentioned above, he was also elected coach of the Singapore Chinese Football Association (SCFA) in early 1949. (He had somehow managed to reconcile with the club that gave him his league debut and where he had starred on numerous occasions.) Lamentably, this stint did not last too long. He controversially stepped down after only six months. According to Seng Quee, some officials of the SCFA had insulted him on numerous occasions. It is unclear whether these insults were due to his training methods or his abrasive manner. But instead of blowing up the matter, he quietly resigned. As he told T. W. Ong, the then President of the SCFA in a semi-official letter, "*I took the insults like a good sportsman for the sake of the Chinese Community XI.*"

Whether it was misfortune or through his own doing, controversy was to follow him throughout his coaching career in Singapore. He had a rocky relationship with SAFA and later with FAS. From his first appointment in 1949 to his eventual departure in 1977 after securing the Malaysia Cup for Singapore, he experienced numerous occasions of conflicts with the football authorities in Singapore.

His first clash with SAFA came in 1949, when he was critical of the association. In an article in *The Sunday Tribune* on 18 September 1949, he lamented that SAFA had done little to bring Singapore's football standards to a more favourable one. He added that unless prodded, the body was reluctant to keep on the move.

This was to be the first of a series of disagreements that Seng Quee had with the footballing authorities that ruled over Singapore football. More were to come in the 1960s and 1970s but we shall leave this for later.

Though Seng Quee's first stint as Singapore coach ended in defeat in the semi-finals of the Malaya Cup, it convinced the Indonesian national team that he was the right person to take the Indonesian team to the next level.

First foreign football coach of Indonesia

It is said that travelling broadens the mind. That is true for everyone, whatever their profession. It was certainly the case for Seng Quee. His view on how the game should be played might have been forged in Singapore, but being exposed to many cultures, new ideas, and new worlds served to broaden his horizons and polish his ideas. He must have witnessed first-hand the game growing and developing everywhere he went.

Being able to harness so many different perspectives opened his eyes in a way that, perhaps, would not have happened had he remained in one place. And it was in Indonesia that Seng Quee had his first taste of being a football coach in a foreign country.

He was also the first foreign coach ever appointed by the Indonesia national team. However, it was an honorary position (a post he would hold from 1949 until 1953) which allowed him to continue coaching at club level in Singapore.

Seng Quee's reputation as a tough taskmaster had caught the attention of an entrepreneur, Tony Wen, who was also in charge of the Football Association of Indonesia in the early 1950s. Tony Wen or Boen Kim To, as he was also known, came from Bangka, the home of Seng Quee's forefathers. He approached Seng Quee with an offer of becoming the national coach of Indonesia. Seng Quee readily accepted the offer.

The Indonesian team had hit a 'high', when playing under the banner of the 'Dutch East Indies', they qualified for the 1938 World Cup thus becoming the first Asian country to play in a World Cup. But their foray on the world stage was a relatively short one as they were eliminated after the first game. Their fortunes went south after that. By the end of the 1940s after securing independence, the team were in the doldrums.

Seng Quee's appointment in 1949 was seen as an attempt to recover some of their past glory. Tony agreed to pay his salary during his tenure with the national team.

Seng Quee's first task was to prepare the Indonesian team for the Asian Games in New Delhi in 1951.

There were only six teams participating in the competition and each game lasted only 60 minutes. Things did not get off to a flying start for Seng Quee. In the opening match, the Indonesian team suffered a heavy defeat against host nation India losing by three goals to nil which meant they were eliminated from the competition. India eventually went on to win the gold medal for the first time in their history. They secured a famous victory against a highly fancied Iranian team in a match that was played before their Prime Minister, Jawaharlal Nehru.

Following their surprise early exit from the 1951 Asian Games, the Indonesian team embarked on a 20-day tour of Manila, Hong Kong and Bangkok. Perhaps the Indonesian team were hoping to recover some lost pride after their 'debacle' in the Asian Games.

Preparations for this tour were intense with a two-week intensive training programme lined up. His gruelling training sessions proved to be unpopular and some of the so-called 'star players' decided to sit out the tour. But Seng Quee, never one to be intimidated by 'star players', gladly replaced them with some reserve players who were only too happy to participate in the tour.

The tour was a great success with the Indonesian team only losing one of the nine games and scoring a hefty 56 goals in the process.

Foremost among their achievements were three straight victories over professional Hong Kong teams. They beat Hong Kong Interport 4-1, Hong Kong Selection 3-2, and the Hong Kong Combined Chinese 5-1 These were some of the top-ranked teams in Asia at that time. Before this, no visiting team had beaten Hong Kong teams three matches in a row.

During Seng Quee's four-year stint as the Indonesian coach from 1949 to 1953, football in Indonesia rose to tantalising heights and saw Indonesia emerging as one of the top teams in Asia under his guidance.

Many Indonesian football greats were produced by Seng Quee, like Ramang from Macassar who was later hailed as the best centre-forward Indonesia has ever produced. In addition, there were Ramlan, Teh San Liong, Jiamiap Dahlar and Tan Liong Hwa.

Many Indonesians still harbour the view that the Indonesian team under Seng Quee was the best in Indonesia's football history.

According to Aqwam Fiazmi Hanifan, who wrote the article, 'Uncle Choo dan Latihan Fisik Timnas Era 1950-an' (Uncle Choo and National Team Physical Exercise 1950s), Seng Quee's regimental training methods were new territory for many of the players in the Indonesian team during that period. But they proved effective and only served to strengthen the team.

Seng Quee left the Indonesian team to return back to Singapore in 1953 but his legacy was felt long after he had departed the Indonesian archipelago.

After his departure, the Indonesian squad that were groomed by Seng Quee continued on their ascending route. In the 1954 Asian Games, they defeated the reigning champions, India, thus avenging their defeat in the 1951 Asian Games, but lost the following round to the eventual winners, the Republic of China (ROC).

They reached their pinnacle in 1956 when they qualified for the 1956 Olympic Games in Melbourne, Australia. At the Games, the Indonesian team came face to face with Russia who had the legendary Lev Yashin in goal. They played above themselves and managed to hold the Russians to a goalless draw. In the replay, however the Russians outplayed the Asian underdogs winning comfortably by four goals without any in reply.

Seng Quee's contributions to Indonesian football did not go unnoticed. In 1982, at a special ceremony in Jakarta to commemorate the 50th anniversary of the Indonesian Football Federation, the Federation conferred upon Seng Quee the First Class Gold Medal for his contribution to the development of Indonesian football.

And in several internet websites in Indonesia, he was selected as one of the five best coaches that the Indonesian national team ever had. That honour would have pleased Seng Quee coming from a place where his forefathers originated from.

Tunku's pride

Seng Quee's success in transforming the Indonesian national team from perennial strugglers into a formidable force caught the attention of many national teams. It was only a matter of time before another offer would come.

Across the Causeway, Tunku Abdul Rahman Putra Al-Haj ibni Almarhum Sultan Abdul Hamid Halim Shah (or Tunku Abdul Rahman or simply 'Tunku'), the then Prime Minister of Malaya and also President of the Football Association of Malaya (FAM), was setting his sights on taking Malayan football onto the global stage.

The Tunku was passionate about football. He might have acquired this keen interest while studying in the UK. When he became head of FAM in 1951, his vision was to lead Malayan football into a new phase. The FAM had been inducted as one of 14 founding members of the AFC in 1956. They then became a full-fledged member of FIFA in 1958.

What he needed next was a football coach who shared his vision of success and top of his list was Choo Seng Quee. He got his prized catch in January 1958 when Seng Quee was appointed coach of Malaya. Under the terms of his contract, he was to coach the Malayan national team and hold coaching clinics for the Malay states. He was paid a monthly salary of $700 plus free accommodation and travelling expenses.

By now, football had consumed Seng Quee. He wanted to remain as close as possible to football. In 1958, he made the bold decision to become a professional coach, something which was unheard of during that period. While others were content on playing or coaching football and having another job to supplement their income, Seng Quee's vision was to 'live and breathe' football!

This actually worked to the FAM's favour as they had a plan to conduct a nation-wide coaching clinic to search for the best players to represent Malaya in the 1958 Asian Games. He became a sought-after man as the various states scrambled to secure his services to conduct clinics for the respective states.

His coaching clinics normally consisted of two sessions; one from 6.30am to 7.30am, and another from 5pm to 7pm. These sessions also included other coaches who were keen to learn from the 'maestro'. As many as 70 players from different clubs participated in each of these highly anticipated sessions.

Seng Quee's first match in charge of the Malayan team was, ironically, against Singapore on 2 March 1958 which ended in a 5-2 victory for Malaya.

For the preparation of the Malayan team for the Asian Games, the FAM decided to engage an English coach to work with Seng Quee. Throughout his career, Seng Quee was often tasked with working along with another coach. Ronald Meades came with outstanding credentials having coached the Indian and Pakistani national teams and was recommended by Sir Stanley Rous, the then secretary of the English Football Association.

Meades, who arrived on a two-week contract, was impressed by the fitness levels of the players. Seng Quee had been entrusted with the task of ensuring that his players were able to match the physical prowess of their much stronger opponents.

However, the Malayans failed to impress in the Asian Games and were eliminated from the competition after suffering defeats to Vietnam and China, the eventual winners during the group stages.

But the Tunku kept his faith in Seng Quee. And this trust did not go unrewarded. Seng Quee's next challenge was the Merdeka Tournament. The Merdeka Tournament (or the Merdeka Anniversary Football Festival as it was sometimes known as) was created to commemorate the Independence Day in Malaysia. The games were played at the newly created Merdeka Stadium.

The Merdeka Stadium with its 45,000 capacity was Tunku's 'baby'. He had a vision of having a larger stadium so that more people would be able to watch the Malayan team in action. His dream was realised in time for him to announce the formal declaration of independence of the Federation of Malaya on 31 August 1957. How many of us can forget his shouts of 'Merdeka' in this magnificent venue?

And it was at the 1st Merdeka Tournament that Seng Quee had his first taste of victory with the Malayan team. Five territories took part in the 1958 tournament which was organised in a round-robin format where all the teams played against each other. Under Seng Quee's leadership, the Malayan team led by captain Chan Tuck Choy won their opening match of the tournament against Indonesia. The Indonesian team who had secured the bronze medal in the Asian Games held a few months earlier were one of the favourites to win the tournament. The Malayans followed up on this success with victories against Hong Kong and South Vietnam. They only failed to win against Seng Quee's home country, Singapore, with the match finishing goalless. With three victories and one draw, the Malayans topped the group and hence claimed the Merdeka Cup.

Shortly after their victory in the 1958 Merdeka Tournament, Seng Quee's courted controversy with the FAM. He was censured by the FAM for writing four articles without FAM's approval.

Journalists looking for a story often turned to Seng Quee hoping to find one and the attention-seeking coach gladly obliged on numerous occasions. He contributed four articles to *The Straits Times* in 1959. The articles were 'A soccer revolution for Malaya needed', 'The plan for our youth', 'Footballers should accept criticism as a spur to better efforts', and 'Tactics for Malayan footballers were the thoughts of a football visionary'. Anyone reading these articles would immediately identify that here was a man who understood the ins and outs about football and was able to come up with a plan to elevate the status of Malayan football.

The FAM, unfortunately, were not keen to see their coach express his thoughts and ideas to the general public. Though the articles were not critical of anyone, the FAM alleged that he had breached his contract as he did not obtain permission from them to communicate with the press. His position at FAM seemed to be under threat as they pondered on what action to take against Seng Quee. They even considered having a new coach.

One of those who applied for the possible vacant position was Frank Soo, an Englishman, who became the first English player of Chinese origin to represent England when he donned the English colours against Ireland and Wales in 1946.

Fortunately for Seng Quee, the FAM opted only to censure him for writing those four articles and he retained his position as coach of the Malayan team. However, they decided not to send him on a planned coaching course to the UK. Whether it was a retribution for his actions, we can only speculate. However, that coaching course to the UK would come two years later. We will get to that shortly.

With this unnecessary distraction out of the way, Seng Quee was able to focus his attention on preparing the Malayan team to defend their Merdeka Cup.

Datuk M. Kuppan clearly remembers Seng Quee as a "*very strict man*" during their centralised training sessions. Kuppan holds the distinction of having won the champion's medal in the Merdeka Tournament as both a player (1958, 1959, and 1960) and coach (1976). According to Kuppan, "*The coach (Seng Quee) had his own way of doing things. He did not like us to take afternoon naps, so he would do daily rounds to check on us. He also checked the bathroom from time to time to see if anyone had been smoking.*"

Malaya started their defence of the Merdeka Tournament in 1959 with a 4-3 win over South Vietnam. The team then drew 1-1 with India before a 2-1 win over Hong Kong confirmed them as champions.

Nine teams took part in the 1960 Merdeka Tournament. Malaya began with a 3-0 win over Japan. An 8-2 defeat of Thailand and a one-goal win over Pakistan followed. Malaya shared the trophy with South Korea after a goalless draw in the final.

Hence it was three Merdeka Cup victories out of three for Seng Quee. For the Tunku, his faith in Seng Quee had paid off in the best possible manner. Seng Quee's role had been mainly to shore up the fitness of the players while the second coach's role was more tactical. But since many of the second coaches like Ronald Meades and former Bolton Wanderers player Harold Hassall only had short-term contracts of around two weeks, it was Seng Quee who had a greater influence on the players.

Seng Quee's success with the Malayan team in the Merdeka Tournaments did not escape the eyes of many suitors. Offers for work came flooding in.

In 1959, Seng Quee received an offer from the Japanese national team to become their coach. Dr. Soichi Ichida, Director of the Japanese Football Federation invited Seng Quee to coach the Japanese team for two months. He believed that Seng Quee could do a lot to improve their players.

Japanese football had taken a backseat after the Second World War due to the country's isolation from the rest of the world. It was only in 1950 that Japan was allowed to rejoin FIFA.

Dr. Ichida was impressed with the Malayan team's fighting spirit and teamwork when the Japanese team did a tour in Malaysia in 1958 and was of the view that such qualities in the team could only be due to the man behind the scene — the coach. But Seng Quee politely turned down the lucrative offer from the Japanese team, preferring to focus his attention on further strengthening the Malayan team.

The Japanese, disappointed by Seng Quee's rejection pursued in their search for an experienced coach and eventually appointed the

German coach Detmar Cramer. (Cramer is commonly considered to be the father of modern football in Japan and coached the Japanese team at the 1964 Olympic Games in Tokyo where they secured a famous 3-2 victory over Argentina. They also grabbed the bronze medal at the 1968 Olympic Games.) Who knows; Seng Quee could have been the one to be dubbed the 'Father of modern Japanese football' had he taken up the offer from Dr. Ichida!

Seng Quee's contract with the FAM terminated in January 1961. But he had done enough to convince the FAM to offer him a two-year contract extension which he gratefully accepted. Added to that, they also rewarded Seng Quee's loyalty and his efforts to upgrade the level of football in Malaysia by sending him on a six-month coaching course in England. The trip was personally arranged by the Tunku with a British Council bursary.

While he was in the UK, arrangements were also made for Seng Quee to be attached to Burnley Football Club, the English league champions at that time. He also had short spells with two other English First Division clubs, Everton and Sheffield United. Seng Quee departed for the UK on 25 January 1961.

The UK adventure

Arriving in the UK in the heart of winter may not have been the ideal introduction to English football. Seng Quee's first port of call was Burnley Football Club. Burnley was a small Lancashire club from the north of England with a rich footballing tradition. It was founded in 1882. When Seng Quee arrived at Burnley, they were the reigning Division One champions of England. They had won the First Division championship in 1960. They secured the championship on the last match day of the season with a 2-1 victory at Manchester City. With 80,000 inhabitants, Burnley became one of the smallest towns to win the league.

While at Burnley Football Club, he was given the royal treatment. He had the honour of being invited as a guest to the seaside resort town of Brighton where Burnley were preparing for their Fourth Round FA Cup match against Brighton & Hove Albion. That game ended in a 3-3 draw, with Burnley overcoming their stubborn Second Division rivals 2-0 in the replay.

He was then invited to visit Germany with Burnley for their second leg of the European Cup quarter-final match against Hamburg SV. Burnley were competing in their first-ever European Cup competition having won their league the season before. The Hamburg team was led by the great German football legend, Uwe Seeler. Seeler who played in the losing West German team in the 1966 World Cup final in England, was named by Pele as one of FIFA's 125 greatest living players in 2004.

Apart from Burnley, Seng Quee was also attached to Sheffield United and Everton. Of the three clubs, he was quite impressed by Everton. He was confident that they would do great things in the following season. (Everton did in fact win the First Division championship two seasons later in 1963 and went on to win another league title in 1970. They also won the FA Cup in 1966.)

Seng Quee must have made quite an impression during his stint in the UK. *The London Sunday Times* of 26 February 1961 made the following remark about him:

"Choo Seng Quee is a large plump chuckling Malayan who knows more about British football than most British footballers. He's wonderfully well informed on world football, can demonstrate

a Stanley Matthews feint, with agility remarkable in one so large and firmly believes in relaxation."

According to Harry Potts, the manager of Burnley Football Club, Seng Quee had *"high praise from all quarters"*.

Even Jimmy Mcllroy, who was at that time playing for Burnley Football Club, and dubbed the 'Brain of Burnley', decided to adopt Seng Quee's diet method of eating more carbohydrates rather than solely relying on proteins which was the favoured diet regime of English footballers.

John Harris, the former Chelsea and Scottish centre-half and manager of Sheffield United in 1961, wrote of Seng Quee in the Sheffield sports paper *Star Green 'Un*:

"During my talks with him (Seng Quee), I soon discovered the thorough knowledge and deep understanding of football he possesses — qualities I had not previously associated with Malayan football. He has obviously studied soccer from every possible angle and is prepared to travel to every corner of the world in order to increase his knowledge."

The *Burnley Evening Telegraph* on 25 March 1961 said after interviewing him:

"Mr. Choo is a man with a vast knowledge of soccer coaching, training and club organisation."

Indeed the newspaper was so impressed that they invited Seng Quee to write a series of articles giving his observations and hints on football.

Still in the UK in May 1961, Seng Quee managed to pull some strings to obtain a precious ticket for the 1961 FA Cup final. For many, trying to secure an FA Cup final ticket was an impossible exercise. The final saw Tottenham Hotspurs beat Leicester City by two goals to nil. Thus, they became the first club to secure the famous 'Double' in the 20th century. (They had already clinched the First Division title a couple of weeks earlier.)

But Seng Quee was disappointed with the match. In an interview given to journalists a few months later, he lamented that it was far from a brilliant match. He felt that Spurs did not really settle down to play their best football. It was only after Leicester City had been reduced to 10 men (after an injury to full-back Len Chalmers) that their performance improved. (Substitutes were still not allowed in 1961 even if the team had a player injured, unless it was the goalkeeper. The first substitutes were only introduced in 1965.)

Of all the concepts and ideas that Seng Quee picked up from the three clubs, the one concept that struck Seng Quee very forcibly was their emphasis on the quality of training rather than the number of hours put in. Seng Quee was also impressed by the emphasis on blind side passing.

Seng Quee took the opportunity to meet as many people associated with football as possible, during his trip to the UK. He met Sir Stanley Rous, the then secretary of the Football Association in England who later served as President of FIFA from 1961 to 1974. During their meeting, he presented gifts to Sir Stanley which were from the Malayan Prime Minister, Tunku Abdul Rahman.

In turn, Sir Stanley presented Seng Quee with a leather wallet bearing the FA crest and the FA badge.

During his conversation with Sir Stanley, Seng Quee cheekily remarked that he was amazed at the leniency shown by British referees. He said, "*In my country the tactics of some of the players here would not be tolerated. There would be stern disciplinary action by the referee.*"

Sir Stanley, who himself was a former referee and officiated the 1934 FA Cup final, diplomatically agreed with Seng Quee's opinion.

Among the other illustrious football personalities that Seng Quee had the fortune to exchange ideas with was Walter Winterbottom, the English FA's chief coach and team manager of the England international team. Walter Winterbottom (later to become Sir Walter) was considered by many to be 'The Father of Modern English Football'. He was a pioneer of coaching and a visionary who made this philosophy the cornerstone of his work. It must have been a great exchange between these two highly enlightened coaches.

In total, Seng Quee witnessed more than 20 football matches, travelling with the Burnley team by plane, coach and train to all their matches.

In an interview with British journalist Doug Lackersteen, Seng Quee commented that he was impressed with the work ethic of the English players. He said, "*Over here, the players are a tough forceful crowd who keep at it till the final whistle. English teams contend with all kinds of conditions — sometimes rain and mud turn pitches into 'padi' fields, sometimes the ground is snow-covered or icebound. Players here have amazing stamina and ruggedness.*"

There have been questions as to whether Seng Quee completed any coaching courses while he was in the UK. Justin Morais recalls meeting him once in London but is doubtful that he ever completed any course due to the short length of his stay there and the amount of time he spent with the English clubs.

Seng Quee's six-month stint in England ended on 14 June 1961. But before he returned to Malaya, he was awarded two trophies to be given to the FAM to hold two local football tournaments. The first trophy was to be the Burnley Cup for a football tournament for under-19 players and the second was the Sheffield United trophy for a football tournament for under-15 players.

The Sheffield United trophy did not survive the hands of time but the Burnley Cup became a premier tournament for budding youth footballers in Malaysia and in 1973, the name of the Burnley Cup was changed to the Razak Cup (Piala Razak in Malay), named after Tun Abdul Razak, former FAM President and Malaysian Prime Minister.

Back in Malaya

Seng Quee flew back to Malaya at the end of June 1961 having studied coaching methods with three leading English clubs. His first mission once he was back was to prepare the Malayan team for the Merdeka Tournament in August.

Though they lost the final 2-1 to Indonesia, the Tunku was so pleased with their performance at the tournament that he presented all the players, including Seng Quee with wrist watches. More importantly, the FAM made a profit of almost $30,000 from the tournament.

Soon after their exploits in the Merdeka Tournament, Seng Quee's team was back on the training grounds again hoping to get in shape for a series of matches in Vietnam to commemorate the Vietnam National Day celebrations in Saigon. But the preparations were hindered by absenteeism. Many players did not turn up at the training sessions. Seng Quee was infuriated and tendered his resignation as Malayan national coach in 1961. However, the Tunku persuaded him to continue in his coaching position. Tunku Abdul Rahman declared that his resignation *"will certainly be a calamity to the football fraternity of Malaya"*.

It was easy to see why the Tunku desperately wanted Seng Quee to stay on. Seng Quee had reinvigorated Malayan football. He had kick-started the country's golden age of football. They had won three consecutive victories in the Merdeka Tournament, and were unfortunate to lose to Indonesia in the final of 1961 tournament. The momentum had been generated for more success and the Tunku was convinced that only Seng Quee could steer the team to greater heights.

And the Tunku was proved right. The Malayan team claimed the gold medal at the 1961 South-East Asian Peninsular (SEAP) Games in December 1961.

The first SEAP Games had been held in Bangkok two years earlier. In the football competition, Malaya had clinched the bronze medal and were hoping for more success at the 1961 Games.

During the tournament, Malaya defeated Burma 2-1 and Cambodia 4-0 to top their group. They advanced to the final by virtue of winning the coin toss after a 2-2 draw with Thailand in the semi-finals. Malaya scored two late goals in the final 10 minutes to defeat hosts Burma 2-0 to win the football competition.

At the 1962 Asian Games in Indonesia, Seng Quee's Malayan team finished as the third-best team in Asia after beating South Vietnam 4-1 in the third and fourth placing match. They had been narrowly beaten by South Korea after extra-time in the semi-finals.

Along their way to the semi-finals, they demolished the Philippines 15-1 in a group match. Eleven of the goals in that victory came from Abdul Ghani Minhat. That 15-1 victory is currently the record for the highest win for the Malaysian national team and the record has never been broken ever since.

The Tunku, ever so eager to find ways to improve Malayan football, suggested to the FAM that Seng Quee together with Abdul

Ghani, the top footballer in Malaya at that time, should be sent to Brazil to discover the secrets of Brazil's 'soccer astronauts' as the Brazilian football team was dubbed back then. The Seleção (as the Brazilian team were sometimes known as) were winners of the 1958 World Cup and were preparing to defend their title at the 1962 World Cup in Chile. (They eventually retained their title.) Sadly for both Seng Quee and Ghani, that trip to the land of 'samba football' never took place.

A clearly disappointed Seng Quee was left to reflect on what might have been had he made it to Brazil especially since Brazilian soccer was at its zenith with rising stars like Pele and Mario Zagalo and established geniuses like Didi, Garrincha and Zito.

He put that disappointment behind him and pressed on his next task which was to train and inspire the next generation of Malayan coaches. Many of them were to move on to become successful coaches for their state teams. One of them was Jalil Che Din, who would eventually become the Malaysian coach and lead them to qualification for the 1972 Olympic Games.

Meanwhile, on the political front, a host of events were taking place that would forever change the political landscape. As was mentioned earlier, on 16 September 1963, through a merger, all the Malayan states formed a larger federation called Malaysia together with Singapore, Sarawak and North Borneo.

The merger, which lasted for less than two years, was thought to benefit the economy by creating a common free market, eliminating trade tariffs, and solving unemployment woes. The British government approved the merger, convinced that Singapore's security would be safeguarded within the much larger Malaysia.

However, the alliance was rocky from the start. The merger was undermined by mutual suspicions and by differing notions of what the new state would actually entail. Some politicians exploited the racial imbalance in the two territories. Racial tensions increased dramatically within a year, culminating in the racial riots that first took place on Prophet Muhammad's birthday on 21 July 1964 with 23 people killed and hundreds injured.

The merger between Singapore and Malaya was also mirrored in football. SAFA became affiliated to the renamed Football Association of Malaysia as a state association.

Ironically, for Seng Quee, the period of merger between Singapore and Malaysia meant that he suddenly had a larger pool of players to tap from. For the Malaysian pre-Olympic Games match against Thailand, he had four players in his team who had represented Singapore earlier: Lee Kok Seng, Majid Ariff, Mahat Ambu and Quah Kim Swee.

Seng Quee's contract eventually ended in March 1963 and was not renewed. The FAM had decided that a fresh approach to coaching was needed to help Malayan football keep pace with rising world standards. They felt that the best way to keep right abreast of modern training methods and techniques was to get a coach from Europe.

He was appointed the national schools coach responsible for training and scouting youth players on 1 April. For a man, who had elevated two national teams to regional reckoning, this new post was not what he had envisaged.

However, the press hailed the appointment. Takashi Mori, the President of the Federation of Malaya Schools Sports Council said, *"The appointment of Seng Quee is a move in the right direction. It is only proper that the schools — the nursery of sportsmen — should have a qualified soccer coach."*

Like all the other disappointments he had faced before, Seng Quee took it in his stride. He mapped out an ambitious eight-month tour covering all states to give football instruction to teachers and schoolboys. In the interim, he was also tasked with preparing the Malayan youth team for the Junior Asian Cup competition.

The FAM had set their hopes on appointing a German coach to take over the reins from Seng Quee. However, the coach that they had in mind decided to accept another coaching offer. The Tunku had once again turned to his 'favourite son' and announced Seng Quee would coach Malaysia for the two preliminary round matches of the Olympic Games, the Aga Khan Cup in Dacca, Pakistan in late October as well as the Asian Cup Central Zone ties in Saigon in November 1963.

But despite being eliminated from the pre-Olympic Games competition as well as limited success in the Aga Khan Cup and Asian Cup ties, Seng Quee was optimistic that a Malaysian football revival was around the corner. His aim was to return Malaysian football to the heydays of the late 1950s. But deep down, he knew that his days with the Malaysian team were nearing its end. It was no open secret that the Malaysians were still in the hunt for a new coach.

After a three-month coaching spell in Singapore which culminated in Singapore winning the Malaya Cup in 1964, he headed back to Malaysia. He was convinced once again that his 'mojo' was working. However this time, he was left to train a young and inexperienced Malaysian team for the Merdeka Tournament. Despite handing the defending champions, Nationalist China (Formosa), a 5-2 thrashing, they were unable to replicate their success against the other teams and were eventually eliminated from the competition.

Despite their failure in the competition, the Tunku was pleased as the competition had generated a profit of almost $70,000 for the FAM. He was also glad that the competition went on, despite the shadow of the 'Indonesian confrontation' hanging above them. (The Indonesian confrontation or '*Konfrontasi*' in Indonesian/Malay was a violent conflict that stemmed from Indonesia's opposition to the creation of the Federation of Malaysia.)

Though Seng Quee was to continue with his role as a Malaysian schools coach after the Merdeka Tournament, he decided to return to Singapore. In an interview given to journalist Joe Dorai in 1965, Seng Quee expressed his frustration with his schoolboy coaching role. He also disclosed that it was taking a toll on his health. The job required him to work nine to 10 hours a day and that his poor health did not allow him to carry out his duties to his full satisfaction. He also added that after each Merdeka Tournament, he was entitled to a vacation but after the last vacation he saw no point in returning to coach the schools as the school holidays had already started. And when the school holidays were over, the fasting month had begun.

The FAM was incensed by his absence. A spokesman of the FAM said that Seng Quee left Malaysia after the Merdeka Tournament without informing anyone. They wrote to him asking if he was still interested in the schoolboy coaching role. Seng Quee did not respond. Another letter was sent by the FAM informing Seng Quee that since he had not responded to their previous letter, it could be construed that he was no longer keen on working with the Malaysians. Thus ended his long-standing relationship with the Malaysian team.

Seng Quee cherished his coaching stint with the Malaysian team. He had said on numerous occasions that the Malaysians were fortunate to have the Tunku as the head of the Malaysian football body because of his dedication to Malayan football. In defeat and victory, the Tunku, according to Seng Quee *"kept a level head"*.

Seng Quee was proud of what he had done for Malayan football. At an interview after the announcement to appoint a new coach was made, he said, *"I am satisfied I did my best with the limited opportunities I had with the national team. After all, I never had the team under me for more than three weeks at a time before international events and that is a very short time."*

In total, Seng Quee spent slightly more than five years in Malaysia, his longest spell with a country or club.

Chapter Seven

Seng Quee: Stamping His Mark as Singapore's Legendary Coach

Singapore coach once again

After 15 years in the wilderness, Seng Quee was coach of Singapore once more. He had contacted the Singapore Amateur Football Association (SAFA) to train the Singapore team in April 1964. His request fell on deaf ears but a month later, SAFA decided to appoint Seng Quee as Singapore's coach. His contract was for a period of three months to train the Singapore team for the 1964 Malaya Cup. While coach of Malaysia, Seng Quee had expressed his desire to train the team of his land of birth on several occasions.

It remains a mystery why SAFA waited 15 years before reappointing him again. During those interim years, Seng Quee had proved his mettle while working with the Indonesian and Malaysian teams. He proved that he could raise a team, put them through several weeks of intensive training and then get them to perform wonders in tournaments. Was it due to his 'larger than life' personality and his habit of wanting to have things done his way that prevented an earlier appointment?

There was no fanfare when Seng Quee arrived back in Singapore. It was business as usual. His second spell as Singapore coach (the first being in 1949) was to be for only three short months.

His first task was to get the players in shape for the Aw Hoe Cup interport matches against Hong Kong. Things got off to a flying start for Seng Quee. Under the guidance of captain, Lee Kok Seng, Singapore beat their fancied rivals 2-1 in the replay (following a 1-1 draw) to claim the Aw Hoe Cup in July 1964. In the interim, the Singapore Malays team also clinched the Sultan's Gold Cup. Winning the Malaya Cup final the following month which Singapore had qualified for would have given them a hat trick of cups. Standing in their way for this famous 'triple' were the hard men from Perak. The Perak team included former Singapore centre-forward, Mahat Ambu, who had moved to Perak in 1961. He eventually returned to the Singapore team in 1965.

Having defeated Perak in the final four years earlier, the Singapore team was in a confident mood. Their road to the final had been a relatively easy one as for the first time since 1958, their arch-rivals, Selangor, were not in their group having been drawn into the north zone. Singapore qualified easily for the final with three games to spare. For this final, they had two advantages over Perak — their experience and their solid defence.

The 1964 final will long be remembered as the 'Rahim Omar's Final'. He was Singapore's danger man and grabbed two goals which saw Singapore edge Perak 3-2. This included an excellent 'banana kick' in extra time which sealed Singapore's victory. Singapore had earlier forced the game to go into extra-time with a last-minute header by defender Lee Wah Chin.

The game was also remembered for the minute's silence before the game in memory of Awang Bakar, the great Singapore centre-forward who had passed away in early July that year after a fall during a friendly match. Seng Quee had paid tribute to Awang Bakar saying, *"His death is a great loss to Singapore football."*

Though Seng Quee's contract ended, he once again offered to coach Singapore in early 1965. In addition to a monthly wage, he made an unusual request for a share of the gate receipts.

SAFA seemed puzzled by this bizarre request. But he gave them the assurance that he could raise the Singapore team again to the level of their former 'golden days' and bring the crowds back to the Jalan Besar Stadium. The fact that SAFA would benefit in every way if this were to happen, made the finance committee of SAFA well disposed towards Seng Quee's strange proposal.

In February 1965, they agreed to offer Seng Quee a contract of a monthly wage of $250 plus a cut of the gate receipts. He was to also spearhead a coaching panel of 10 coaches whose task would be to form five reserve state training squads to provide the Singapore team with a continuous supply of coached players.

In addition, he was also given the role of talent spotter, something SAFA recognised he was good at when he was coaching the Singapore team for the Malaya Cup a year ago.

While Seng Quee's role was to coach the team, the selection of the players for the team was made by a panel of selectors. The selectors were all part of SAFA, led by SAFA President, Hussein Kamari. Hussein had been unanimously elected president for a third consecutive term in January 1965. However, his third term was wrought with tough challenges. One of them was the problem of absenteeism of players for training sessions. Many of the players had full-time day jobs and the perennial problem was getting leave from their employers for training and matches. The situation got so bad that SAFA was forced to have a meeting in October to address the issue. The Singapore team was competing in the South-East Asian Peninsular (SEAP) Games for the first time as an independent nation. The selectors were keen to see Singapore perform well and the absenteeism issue most certainly did not help in their quest to achieve this goal.

However, this is not the biggest issue that Hussein Kamari faced. On 2 September 1965, 28 football clubs petitioned SAFA calling on the 24-man council to resign en-bloc. They accused the SAFA council of gross mismanagement of the association's affairs.

The move was initiated when SAFA decided not to participate in the SEAP Games and instead focus on the interport match in Hong Kong. Hussein saw the issue as two camps within SAFA bidding for power. A vote of no confidence was passed. Hussein tendered his resignation and Abu Bakar Pawanchee, who was then the permanent secretary to the Foreign Ministry, became the new President of SAFA.

For Seng Quee, he had to put the internal turmoil within SAFA as well as the political squabbles between Singapore and Malaysia behind him. His mind was focussed on Singapore retaining the 1965 Malaya Cup as well as the Aw Hoe Cup. He had to deal with a squad composed of players of different races who were still feeling the after-effects of the racial riots, especially the Chinese and Malay players.

The Singapore team did well to retain the Malaya Cup, defeating Selangor 3-1 in the final. Those who watched the game dubbed it as the 'Majid Ariff Final'. But those in the back room knew it was equally appropriate to call it the 'Choo Seng Quee Final'.

Seng Quee's calibre as a master tactician was for all to see during this final. Seng Quee's plan was simple: contain Selangor until the last 15 minutes. All that was required of Singapore was possession football and conservation of energy.

The game went according to plan. Selangor 'huffed and puffed' against a solid Singapore wall. Selangor did take the lead after 57 minutes. But by then, they were already showing signs of extreme fatigue.

The Singapore comeback was sparked by a wonderful solo effort by the legendary Majid Ariff with 17 minutes remaining. Two further goals from Quah Kim Swee (one of the legendary Quah brothers) capped a fine victory for the Singapore team. Even the West German coach of Selangor, Otto Westphal, admitted that Selangor were defeated by a much fitter Singapore team.

Seng Quee added more silverware to the SAFA trophy cabinet when the Singapore team clinched the Aw Hoe Cup for the second year in a row. They defeated a Hong Kong team featuring several professional players by two goals to one in a replay. (The first match ended in a draw.)

Next in line was the SEAP Games in Kuala Lumpur. (The Games were originally scheduled to be held in Laos. However, the Laotians ran into financial difficulties and the games were moved to Malaysia.) While the former SAFA council had agreed to sit out of this competition, the new council were keen to have Singapore participate as a newly independent nation.

Sadly, the preparations were marred by absenteeism. The Singapore team performed dismally at the Games. They lost their first two games losing 1-0 to Burma before receiving a 5-1 thrashing from South Vietnam. Then, to everyone's surprise, they pulled out of the tournament. No reasons were given. As a result, the remaining group matches were cancelled.

Following the competition, SAFA dropped a bombshell on 28 December 1965. It was announced in the media that SAFA had sacked Seng Quee with immediate effect. Six players were also dropped from the national team. They were captain Quah Kim Swee, Mokhtar Tabri, Majid Ariff, Quah Kim Siak, Ali Astar and Mahat

Ambu. Their offence: alleged misconduct and insubordination at the 1965 SEAP Games.

In the official team report, team manager Tan Peng Gee alleged that Seng Quee *"was being difficult from the very moment the team arrived in Kuala Lumpur from Hong Kong"*. Seng Quee was accused of not following the manager's instructions and inciting resentment and undisciplined behaviour of the team in general. Tan Peng Gee in his report to SAFA accused Seng Quee and six players of misconduct and insubordination.

Tan Peng Gee in his report also claimed that the captain, Quah Kim Siak, had demanded allowances before the tournament was scheduled to start and the other players had followed this line.

In another *The Straits Times* article from 29 December 1965, it was alleged that SAFA had been giving their players a bonus of $100 for a win in addition to a regular $15 'pocket money' for every international match. The new council wanted to put an end to this practice as all the players were purely 'amateurs' and were not expected to receive payments. There is a strong possibility that the plan by the council to stop making payments was not conveyed to the players. Hence, they should not be faulted for making a 'normal' demand.

Nevertheless, the SAFA council decided to drop the six players from the national team training squad. The council also decided that Seng Quee would cease to be a coach with immediate effect as a result of the charges made against him by Tan Peng Gee.

Seng Quee was shocked by the action taken by SAFA. He sent a letter to SAFA. In his letter, he claimed that SAFA could not pass judgment on him and the players and the council's decision should be treated as null and void. The allegations had to be investigated before action was taken.

Seng Quee and the six 'dropped' players requested for an independent inquiry by the Singapore Olympic and Sports Council (SOSC) or the National Sports Council (NSC) to clear their names. He pleaded, *"I feel I should be given the chance to clear myself and an independent inquiry should be appreciated by myself and the players concerned."* This request failed and both the SOSC and NSC considered the matter to be an internal one and refused to interfere.

Apputhurai Thurai Rajah, the then President of the SOSC, did state that as SAFA was affiliated to the council, they could write to the SOSC if they wished and the SOSC would then advise them on how to deal with the matter. These were not very comforting words for the already alienated Seng Quee.

The decision to sack Seng Quee and ban the six players was not a popular one. Attendances fell for the following five matches against teams from Czechoslovakia and Yugoslavia.

A month later, Seng Quee made a fresh appeal, this time to Bakar Pawanchee, the President of SAFA, to appoint a commission of inquiry to look into the allegations of misconduct. In his own words, he said that he was not *"in the least bothered"* about himself being reappointed as the Singapore coach but he was making this appeal for the welfare of Singapore soccer. He was more concerned that the banned players be given a chance to have their say. Yet, once again, his appeal fell on deaf ears.

Undeterred by this sacking, Seng Quee made a fresh offer to coach the national team only six months later. He was prepared to *"let bygones be bygones"* and start on a fresh footing.

There were conflicting reports in the media over his request to take charge of the Singapore team again. A newspaper report on 23 June 1966 reported that a Football Association of Singapore (FAS) official had approached him to become the Singapore coach. However, two days later, the FAS President, Inche Abu Baker Pawanchee, denied that there was such an approach. Instead, the FAS appointed Len Briggs, the coach of the Joint Services Malaya Cup squad, to assist Singapore coaches Harith Omar and Abdul Rahman to prepare the team for the 1966 Merdeka Tournament.

This time, the FAS strangely cited a lack of funds to pay his salary as the reason for refusing to engage Seng Quee. They did offer Seng Quee a token sum of $10 per month to maintain his professional status.

In an interview given by Seng Quee in 1975, he admitted that one of the main stumbling blocks over his appointment as coach was Richard Basil Ivor Pates (more popularly known as R. B. I. Pates). Pates was an ex-Southampton football player who also coached the Singapore national team from 1950 to 1959 and was also the Chairman of FAS from 1974 to 1976. Seng Quee claimed that Pates refused to discuss the subject of his appointment at council level.

Hence for the first time since 1958, Seng Quee did not have a national coaching position. He watched in envy while Yap Boon Chuan, a certified British Football Association coach, led Singapore to a credible fourth-placed position at the 1966 Asian Games football competition.

However, it may not have been all that bad for Seng Quee. He had more time to focus on his sports business. He had set up a sport shop called Maju Jaya at Owen Road. The shop sold sports-related items ranging from football jerseys to football boots and also sports trophies. Seng Quee was known to have donated many trophies for sporting competitions in Singapore. His shop was also known for creating the largest sporting trophy in Asia at that time. It was the Mara Halim Trophy which was six-and-a-half feet tall. The trophy was made up of two-and-a-half kilograms of gold and cost $18,000 at that time. A replica version was also made and both versions were made by Maju Jaya Sports Store.

In addition, Seng Quee may have had time to catch the 1966 World Cup on television in the comforts of his home. This was the first World Cup competition which was broadcast globally though few in Singapore would have had the luxury to see England crowned as world champions at home. At that time, less than 5 percent of Singapore's population owned a television set.

With the free time he had, Seng Quee decided to dedicate his time to grassroots football once again. He trained a team of under 10-year-olds of the Singapore Chinese football team.

But his services were still in demand by other teams. Towards the end of 1966, he received a request from an 'old friend', Captain G. Suppiah, who was the secretary of the Malaysian Armed Forces team. They wanted him to coach the armed forces team. The team had reached the Malaya Cup final for the first time the previous season, narrowly losing 1-0 to Selangor. They had also acquired the services of former Singapore talisman, Rahim Omar. Rahim, who at 32 was approaching the tail end of his illustrious career and was working as an instructor in the Territorial Army.

But SAFA decided to give Seng Quee another opportunity in 1967. He became part of a panel that comprised two other coaches namely, Yap Boon Chuan and G. Suppiah, a Loughborough trained schoolteacher. Yap was in charge of the national team while Suppiah was coach of the youth team. Seng Quee took control over the reserves. However, the position came with quite a number of restrictions. He had to abide by the conditions laid out in a memorandum issued to all Singapore football coaches. The Memorandum stipulated that coaches should abide by the coaching committee's decisions. Added to that, the coaches also had no authority in selection when the teams were on tour.

It must have been hard for the old 'war horse' Seng Quee. He was clearly far more experienced than those in the selection committee. However, like a true professional, he accepted the terms and by the end of March was busy training a squad of 43 reserves players all recommended by him.

The Singapore national team captured the FAM Cup after the 2-1 victory over Selangor. The FAM Cup was a secondary knockout competition that was started in 1951. Singapore's only other victory in the competition was in 1963.

Hence, the dream was on to secure a 'double' when the national team booked their place in the Malaysia Cup final. But that dream was shattered by a courageous Perak team who secured victory in extra-time.

The youth team, under Suppiah, surprised everyone by reaching the semi-finals in the Asian Youth Championship which was held in Bangkok in April. Led by captain Brian Richmond (more about him later), the team defeated the heavily fancied host nation, Thailand, in the quarter-finals but could not overcome the Indonesians in the semi-finals. Two Singapore players, goalkeeper Paul Anthonysamy and centre-forward Kadir Suleiman, were rewarded for their fine performances in the tournament and were selected for the Singapore team competing in the Merdeka Tournament.

While preparations were being made by the Singapore team for the Merdeka Tournament, a surprise decision by Yap Boon Chuan to tender his resignation meant that Seng Quee was back in the fray. The Merdeka Tournament was one tournament where Singapore had scant success.

Despite his intensive training sessions, Seng Quee's men did not rise to the challenge. Singapore ended up as wooden-spoonists in the 10-team competition. The team started off well in the tournament holding the Taiwanese team to a 0-0 draw. However, they lost their remaining three group matches to Indonesia, Burma and South Korea. In the consolation match for ninth and 10th placing, they succumbed to Western Australia despite holding the Aussies to 2-2 at half-time. The match eventually ended 5-3 in favour of the Aussies. The 1967 Merdeka Cup was eventually shared by South Korea and Burma after the final ended in a 0-0 draw.

Following their disappointing performance at the Merdeka Tournament, FAS Council member A. Pancharetnam urged that Singapore should not participate in any overseas competitions. Fortunately, the rest of the Council members did not share this view.

With Seng Quee joining forces with West German coach Dettmar Cramer, the Singapore team made amends by recapturing the Aw Hoe Cup with an impressive 4-0 victory against an experienced Hong Kong team.

Sadly, their fortunes hit rock bottom in the South Vietnam Republic Day Tournament in October. The team lost all their three group matches. They were beaten by South Vietnam (2-0), New Zealand (3-1) and Australia (5-1). In their defence, they claimed that nine of their first team players were injured in the first two games and in their final match against Australia, they only had two regular national players in the team. Sadly, the jury was out and the team were axed from the SEAP Games the following month.

Meanwhile, off the field, several major changes were being made. In his 1968 New Year message to all Singaporean sportsmen and sports associations, Othman Wok, the Minister of Culture and Social Affairs (who was also the President of the SOSC), called for higher standards of performance and organisation. *"We have proved that unification of a nation can be achieved through common objectives and participation in sport"*, he declared.

Oddly enough, he blamed the annual communal competitions between Singapore and Malaysian teams as one of the reasons for the poor football standard in Singapore. He added, *"The continuance of these competitions could have been right when we were part of Malaysia. But it is most improper now and should be discontinued."*

Blame was also laid on the FAS for *"fostering this type of competition"*. Othman Wok suggested a five-point plan which included a redrafting of the FAS constitution to improve football in Singapore.

Not surprisingly, the government replaced the entire administration of the FAS with a team of 23 members consisting mainly of government servants led by Lenny Rodrigo, a lawyer and Member of Parliament. But they recalled three prominent officials from the early 1960s: Lim Yong Liang, Kee Yew Leng and R. B. I. Pates. Yong Liang was Seng Quee's mentor early in his career while Yew Leng had played alongside Seng Quee in the Straits Chinese colours during the 1930s.

However, the bigger and longer lasting change was the decision to pull out of the Malaysia Cup and the FAM Cup. According to Mark Emmanuel in his excellent article, 'The Malaysia Cup: Soccer and the national imagining in Singapore, 1965–1996', *"The effect of Singapore's withdrawal from the Malaysia Cup in 1968 was disastrous for the state of soccer in both nations (Singapore and Malaysia)."* He further added that the financial fallout was considerable as fans declined and many states began the 1969 in debt. The pull-out was a huge blow for Singapore football and to its fans as it was deprived of the excitement and passion that the Malaysia Cup generated.

Seng Quee was unfortunately caught in the middle of this politicking. He had been offered the job to coach the Singapore national football team in early 1968. Desperate for recognition at home, he accepted it readily, describing himself as "*honoured and delighted*" to be back in his homeland. He had admitted on numerous occasions that he was not in favour of Singapore participating in the Malaysia Cup and preferred seeing the national team do battle in regional competitions.

But the Malaysia Cup at least provided Seng Quee with the opportunity to work with the Singapore team. The competition usually started in January or February with the final in August or September. Hence, the pull-out meant that his time with the national team was limited. However, whenever he was not training the national team, he kept himself occupied with coaching teams at club level and there was never a shortage of offers.

Coaching at club level

While Seng Quee achieved success at national level with Singapore, Malaysia and Indonesia, he also found success at club level football.

Many clubs were keen to engage the services of Seng Quee to take advantage of his wealth and knowledge. As was mentioned earlier, his first taste of coaching was at the tender age of 25 when he was offered the coaching position at Chinese Athletic (CA) in 1939.

CA had a humble beginning. When the club was formed, its main objective was to foster relationships and goodwill and to promote football and other branches of sport.

With Seng Quee at the helm, he managed to attract many of his former teammates at the Straits Chinese Football Association (SCFA) to join CA. The club was admitted to the SAFA league in 1941 and became one of the dominant forces of the local club football scene during the periods before and after the Second World War.

Seng Quee emphasised the value of youth and when the CA team won the league in 1949, they had the youngest squad of the league. Many of the players were still schooling or in their teens. Seng Quee was always ready to give a chance to the youngsters and to impart to them all that he knew about football.

Seng Quee was CA's coach until 1952 but it was reported in *The Straits Times* on 19 August 1949 that Seng Quee was elected as honorary coach and advisor for a team called Hotspurs XI, a team of promising young Singapore footballers. The team had been formed earlier that year by Ranjit Singh, a fresh-faced 18-year-old. It even included a certain N. Ganesan who was later to become the Chairman of FAS in the 1970s. However, little is known about Hotspurs XI and how long they were in existence.

For Seng Quee, coaching at club level gave him the opportunity to coach young players. Very often, he volunteered his services whenever the opportunity arose, like in 1952, when he offered his services to coach young players in Colony Boys Clubs.

His motto was, "*Give me the necessary facilities, equipment and time — and I will do the rest.*"

Seng Quee strongly believed that the youth was the key to success for the Singapore team.

In 1959, he said, "*Soccer is a young man's game. In youth, the eyes have fantastic swiftness, limbs are marvellously supple, with powers of resilience and recovery.*"

He lamented the absence of trained coaches in many youth teams and urged SAFA to provide subsidies to youth soccer.

In 1952, Seng Quee became manager and coach of a Second Division team, Star Soccerites, another club he founded. The club had ended seventh in the league the previous season but finished runners-up in 1952 to secure promotion to the First Division. Star Soccerites won the title in 1954 and became the glamour side in the league boasting star players like Rahim Omar, Charlie Chan, and later on, Peter Corthine.

Their dominance continued and on 5 March 1957, the club created a sensation by opening their league season with a record 17-1 win over Royal Engineers Civilian Association. Their star striker, Rahim Omar, got eight of the goals, though the man of the match, according to *The Straits Times* was Peter Corthine (who scored six goals in that match).

Peter Corthine was a British serviceman stationed in Singapore. He was once in the Southampton second team and was slated for the first team before being transferred to Singapore for his military service.

While in Singapore, Corthine trained under Seng Quee and featured regularly in the Star Soccerites team. He had high praise for Seng Quee. In his words, *"Seng Quee is in a class by himself. I strongly believe if Seng Quee was in England he would be wanted by many professional clubs as a coach. Comparing their methods and his, I think he has a wider knowledge, covering continental methods as well as those used in other countries."*

Corthine eventually went on to represent Singapore and excelled in the 1957 Merdeka Tournament finishing as the top scorer with seven goals.

Seng Quee left Star Soccerites in 1957. He joined Marine Department Sports Club, a government services team that participated in the First Division of the Government Services League. Marine Department had finished as runners-up in the league the previous year. They were determined to go one step further and attempt to win the league as well as the Government Services Cup.

Under Seng Quee, they achieved that ambition clinching the First Division title. Their hard work paid off. They had training sessions every Wednesday and Saturday during the league season. Seng Quee emphasised teamwork and his policy of blending youth and experience paid dividends. The team consisted of four Malaya Cup players — Omar Awang, Osman Johan, Ibrahim Mansor and Tahir Abu — plus a host of youth players.

From 1958 to 1964, club football took a back seat. The call had come from the Malaysian team. During the off-peak periods when the Malaysians were not training for any tournaments, Seng Quee was assigned to the various Malaysian states to assist in developing grassroots level football.

With Singapore's exclusion from the Malaysia Cup from 1968 to 1970, they were fewer opportunities for Seng Quee at national level. He intensified his efforts to secure coaching stints with clubs. There was never a shortage of clubs willing to secure his services and the tough coaching methods that came with it. Such was his dedication that many of these stints were on an honorary basis. The clubs who were to benefit from his experience and wisdom included Police Sports Association, Burnley United, Singapore Marble, Tampines Rovers, and Farrer Park.

For the Police team, all it took was four months of training under Seng Quee for them to achieve success. They clinched the 1968 President's Cup defeating a highly fancied Fathul Karib team 3-2 in the final.

Playing in that final for the Police team was Brian Richmond, who was later to find fame as a sports commentator, deejay and master of ceremonies in Singapore.

In an interview with the author, Brian who was once captain of the Singapore youth team and also represented the Singapore national team in several regional tournaments, recalled being first spotted by Seng Quee as a 14-year-old:

> *"I was asked to join Seng Quee's 'Sunday sessions'. On the night before the training session, Seng Quee would soak around 25 footballs (footballs were made of leather back then). In the morning before the training, some of us boys would go to his shop to collect the balls. They would be as heavy as lead and we had to practise kicking the ball from the centre of the field towards the goal."*

During the training sessions with the Police team, Brian recalled always training with a football. In addition to teaching ball techniques, Seng Quee also gave them pointers on how to 'intimidate' opponents.

Special mention must be made about Burnley United. This mystical team which is still spoken of in some football circles in Singapore was the glamour youth team in Singapore in the late 1960s. It was known for churning out a regular flow of players for the national and youth squads.

According to musician Jerry Fernandez, who once played in goal for Burnley United, the team was formed around 1965 by former Singapore football legend Dollah Kassim and his brothers. Dollah managed to rope in Samad Allapitchay, future captain of the Singapore national team, and S. Rajagopal who later dazzled Singapore fans in the 1970s with his amazing 'banana kick' free kicks.

Others like Quah Kim Song and M. Kumar, budding talents from Raffles Institution, soon joined the fray. The team, which trained at Farrer Park, caught the eye of Seng Quee who agreed to coach them. With Seng Quee at the helm, the youthful team clinched the FAS League Division Three championship in 1971.

Offers also came from abroad. In 1973, Seng Quee was offered a coaching job to coach Hong Kong professional First Division club Caroline Hill, who were the Hong Kong Jubilee Cup knockout champions at that time. The offer was for an indefinite period with an annual salary HK$60,000 (S$30,000) with first-class board and lodging, and free transport. Seng Quee said that if he did accept the position, he would only stay in Hong Kong for a year. Despite the lucrative offer, Seng Quee rejected the role. This rejection is just one instance of many which proved that money was never a driving factor in determining Seng Quee's roles.

Seng Quee's coaching philosophy

In 1952, Roger Yue, a journalist of the *Singapore Free Press*, referred to Seng Quee was as *"perhaps Singapore's greatest authority on football"*. Though Seng Quee's first became a coach in 1939, his career as a football coach only took off after the Second World War. So why did a journalist provide such a prestigious accolade to a coach who had perhaps only five years of coaching experience?

The answer may lie in the numerous articles Seng Quee had already contributed to the media. Even as early as 1949, Seng Quee was regularly sprouting his football wisdom to the newspapers. Many of his articles were on football tactics and training methods.

In terms of training methods, Seng Quee was way ahead of his time, compared to other coaches in Asia. While today's professional football teams consist of a backroom staff of dietitians, nutritionists, trainers and physiotherapists, Seng Quee did everything by himself. He was coach, discipline master and psychologist all in one.

His motto at that time was *"Give me the necessary facilities, equipment and time — and I will do the rest."*

According to his own account, given to *The Straits Times* in 1975, Seng Quee said that since 1935, he had coached over 100 players who made the top grade in the South-east Asian region. In 1979, when N. Ganesan organised a meeting for the FAS staff coaches with the hope of improving the Republic's football standards, he highlighted Seng Quee's dedication, enthusiasm and professional attitude as the model for them to emulate.

This is what Seng Quee's vision of what a coach should be (as reported in one of the newspapers in Singapore):

"Besides knowing soccer in all its details, the coach must also have plenty of goodwill and be well-informed of the latest developments in the game.

"He must know the styles of all teams until it is impossible for the opposition to confuse him with an unknown plan of attack and defence.

"A soccer coach is not a teacher but a supervisor. A coach can never bestow upon the players — no matter how young the talent under his instruction — the ability to play football.

"Although you can teach soccer, there is a limit to what tuition and practice can do. One must be born with natural skill.

"A coach must gain the confidence of players too."

Through all the interviews with Seng Quee over the years, one phrase that cropped up frequently was 'hard work'. For him, there was no substitute for hard work. And many of his former players can vouch for the intensity of his training sessions. Seng Quee once asked Pele, the legendary Brazilian footballer, if there was a secret to his greatness. Pele said, *"Yes, sheer hard work"*. Pele added that as he grew older, he had to work much harder at the game. Hence, Seng Quee was simply mimicking what other great players vouched as the key to success.

Finding a time and place for training sessions proved to be an issue at times. As many of the players had daytime jobs, most training sessions were conducted in the evenings. At times, he conducted training sessions along the side-lines of the Jalan Besar Stadium while matches were in progress. On one occasion, an irate referee went up to Seng Quee and told him that his workout was a distraction to players in the competing teams and forced him to stop the training. Without wanting to call an early break, Seng Quee continued the training in a car park outside the stadium, using the street lamps as floodlights!

He sometimes also used the Victoria School pitch for some of his workouts. The only hindrance was that there were no floodlights there and training after 7pm proved to be a challenge.

His training sessions were regimented. In an interview, former national player, Samsuddin Rahmat, recalled the training routine for the Merdeka Tournament in 1971.

"We woke up at 5.50am. We would sing the national anthem followed by 30 rounds around the pitch. Then we would start doing some weights. We would then have breakfast around 10am followed by a break. Training resumed at 2pm with some ball control exercises. In the evening, we would continue with some indoor training."

Discipline was one aspect that was key in Seng Quee's game plan, though over the years, it did not go down too well in many quarters. If there is no discipline off the pitch, there is none on it. He firmly believed that it was important that players learnt to obey authority, behave honourably and maintain good order. *"Discipline in football is necessary if you want to achieve good results"*, Seng Quee always reiterated.

Seng Quee felt that discipline was missing in the players in the post war teams. He once said:

> *"Since I became a professional coach, I have found that something was missing like the good old days before World War II. The old group of players learn to obey authority, behave honourably and maintain in good order not only because the players feel forced to do so, but because they chose to do so. They have been helped to realise that these modes of behaviour are essential for winning teams."*

He was a stickler when it came to discipline. He even went as far as devising a code of conduct for players in the 1970s. Seng Quee's code of discipline (approved by the National Sports Promotion Board and enforced on his players during tours) consisted of the following:

— National players are aware that international football is a hard task. They have to be fit and to be prepared to take knocks in order to succeed.
— The national coach has a very hard task on his shoulders, and it is expected that players should give the coach no trouble by observing the rules and regulations governing the tour.

— Players are not permitted to smoke cigarettes, indulge in alcoholic drinks and must abstain from drinking coffee and carbonated drinks (Note: Habitual smokers are encouraged to cut down their smoking).

— Each player is expected to maintain a high standard of discipline inside and outside the hotel, and on the playing field.

— Players must sacrifice and subdue their own personal interest to the interest of the nation.

— Players must never fight or argue among themselves or get hot-tempered. Perfect harmony must prevail among the players.

— Although the urge to win is essential, it is the spirit in which a game is played that is far more important to actual results.

— Over-eating is very harmful to the players. They must eat just enough and not overfeed themselves. Eating is a necessity not a pastime.

— Players are permitted to go out for short walks after each meal, but are advised to keep in one big group to promote a fine team spirit, which is so essential in a football team.

— They are expected to give full response to the hard training schedules arranged by the coach ungrudgingly with real zest and patriotism to our nation.

— Obedient and hardworking players are normally held in high esteem by the coach. If each player strives to look after himself and abides by the rules and regulations, he is definitely an asset not only to the FAS but also to our nation.

— Shouting will be carried out by the coach on the playing field, and players must not interpret loud shouting as scolding. This shouting of instructions done by the coach is in good faith and not amounting to scolding.
— Players who are lazy and train half-heartedly are enemies to our nation.
— Players will be treated with respect, kindness and fairness by the coach. Breaches of misconduct will not be tolerated by the coach.

Today, some might shudder at the thought of having such a code of conduct imposed on players. But for Seng Quee, it was important that players understood their role and responsibilities as players.

In 1957, his training schedule was based on four points that players had to adhere to:

— Practise self-sacrifice for the interest of the nation.
— Work as a team and devote their time to zealous training.
— Develop punctuality and strict discipline.
— Lead a clean life conducive to fitness.

Seng Quee was aware that strict discipline sometimes created frustration but he also emphasised that players should learn and develop football in a training camp where rigid discipline needed to be imposed on the players. And he was determined that there should be discipline on and off the field. During overseas competitions, strict curfews were imposed on players to return to their rooms by a certain hour. Samsuddin Rahmat recalled an overseas competition where Seng Quee used to sit outside the hotel lift to ensure that players did not

Seng Quee stressed that a coach should not only impart football skills and tactics to players but also teach them discipline and sound moral values.

And when there were lapses in discipline, Seng Quee was not afraid of taking immediate action. During some of the centralised training sessions in Singapore, Seng Quee made the players stay together in a hotel. On one particular occasion, while they were staying at the Sea View Hotel, three players broke the 10.30pm curfew. The following day he told the three culprits to pack up and leave the hotel. "*They cried*", Seng Quee said. "*They got in touch with the other players and they all appeared before me. They asked me to pardon them.*" Seng Quee agreed to pardon them. "*I pardoned them because I'm like a father to them*", Seng Quee added.

Seng Quee was always on the lookout for new training methods. His zest for learning new methods from the European continent led him to acquire books from the former Yugoslavia, Hungary and England. In 1957, on the advice of Billy Wright, the England football captain in the 1950s, Seng Quee purchased a book on soccer tactics. Wright had convinced him that the Russian footballers were the fittest in the world. Unfortunately, the book was in Russian. Hence on 25 March 1957, Seng Quee placed an advertisement in the *Singapore Free Press* requesting for the services of a Russian speaker to translate the book. We wonder if anyone came to offer their assistance to Seng Quee with the Russian book! Such were the lengths at which Seng Quee went to further his knowledge on training methods.

He was a fervent believer in Brazilian 'samba' style football. This is what he said about Brazilian players in an interview in 1975: "*The Brazilian player plays football, always relaxed, never tense, stroking the ball from player to player; this is the hallmark of a ball player, of someone who enjoys the game for its own sake minus the rigidity that bedevils those who have to labour and not play.*" He preferred their short passing style rather than the long balls adopted by the English. Samsuddin Rahmat recalled one incident when Seng Quee jokingly said, "*I can write book after book about Brazilian football but with English football, I will write a book and then throw it away!*"

Psychology also played a key role in his training sessions. Many vouched that he was a master at psychology. He knew how to get the maximum out of his players, 'hammering' them when they needed it, praising them when they deserved it. Lim Tien Jit (or 'Rocky' Lim, as he is known to many of his friends), a former player, remembered how Seng Quee used to speak to players individually during training sessions. "*He made you feel special*", Tien Jit added. "*He knew how to touch the hearts and minds of everyone — players, officials, spectators and reporters.*"

Seng Quee had the ability to instil a sense of camaraderie in all the teams that he had managed. He was a firm believer of 'One for all and all for one'. Quah Kim Song, Singapore's superstar striker during the 1970s, clearly remembers an incident when it was drizzling quite heavily and the players were keen to get back to bed after breakfast. But Seng Quee shamed them, when, punctual as usual, he stood in the rain waiting for the players. Seng Quee then said, "*If you boys want to do well in this tournament, you must be prepared to withstand such things.*"

As he spoke, he was drenched to the skin and tears welled in his eyes. Kim Song said that from then on, they never let him down.

For Seng Quee, the five-minute pep talk with his players in the dressing room before they went on the field was put to good effect on many occasions. He used these precious minutes to its maximum to urge his players to give 100 percent effort and die for each other and for their country in the 90 minutes to come. Then, with their war cry of 'Majulah' or 'Merdeka' in the dressing room, they were off onto the field all charged up and ready for battle.

Football, in Seng Quee's mind, was a simple game. Tactics to him simply meant trying to exploit his team's strengths, and to cover their weaknesses, exploiting their opponents' weaknesses and covering their strengths.

He also believed that the coach must gain the confidence of players. In an interview with the *New Nation*, he recalled a coaching incident in Indonesia in 1946. During a coaching clinic there, he overheard one footballer whispering to his teammate: "*Who is this fat man (Choo Seng Quee)? Does he know how to play football?*"

Ignoring this remark, Seng Quee demonstrated ball-play and the young Indonesian footballers were amazed. After that, they had no more doubts as to who the master was.

It was his strong belief that Singapore should never attempt to produce 'robot footballers' by stamping out originality. As such, in Seng Quee's view, there was a great need to have a quota of 'ball artistes'. Additional space was provided to these players to display their individual talent, though the basic premise of discipline still had to be there. Over the years, players like Rahim Omar, Majid Ariff, Quah Kim Song and Dollah Kassim may fit into this elite category. Some ex-players commented that at times, some players were treated differently from others. This may perhaps have not gone on well with conformist driven Singapore. It may even provide a clue as to why he never had a smooth relationship with both SAFA and FAS who wanted coaches to treat all players alike.

Seng Quee's vision was always hard football but never to resort to dirty tactics. He highlighted this to Selangor before the second leg of the Malaysia Cup semi-final against Selangor in 1977. He said this before the match:

> *"It is not my philosophy to instruct the players to indulge in rough tactics. We believe in skills. My former players, especially those in Malaysia now will tell you that Seng Quee does not coach players to be dirty."*

Seng Quee was all in favour of ball-play. In a column that he regularly wrote for the *New Nation*, a Singapore afternoon newspaper, he emphasised that ball-play must dominate the training schedules. Many coaches in the UK, right up to the 1960s felt that ball-work should be limited during training sessions in order to save the players from getting stale. However, Seng Quee believed that the only way to become a good ball player was by practising with the ball.

Seng Quee was never afraid of trying out different strategies. He was a close disciple of football tactics from different countries. He also kept himself up to date on the latest training methods; he was an avid follower of the Brazilian and English systems.

He was also a great advocate of attacking football. He even was able to get his teams to work on two different sets of tactics depending on what strategy the opposition was using.

What qualities does Seng Quee look for in a player? In one of his regular columns in the *New Nation* on 25 January 1976, Seng Quee said this of the qualities that he expected in a player:

> *"Ball control, sense of intelligent positioning or play without the ball, quickness on and to the ball, strong and sure in the tackle and be able to recover quickly, a 90-minute player, right*

temperament, right approach to the game, cool at all times, willing to learn and to improve his play, and maintain his love for the game."

Criticisms of his coaching methods

Seng Quee experienced great success both at international level and at club level over the years. But there were many who were not in favour of his training methods.

His detractors felt that his methods of training were too rigid for the players who were only amateurs and played football in their spare time. But they did admit somehow that some of the crude methods he used were necessary, especially when it came to fighting against poor discipline from the players.

Over the years, players have complained about his almost 'military-like' training methods.

During a tour of Saigon (now Ho Chi Minh) and Bangkok in 1971, the relationship between Seng Quee and his players hit a new low. There was talk of rebellion among the players due to enforced schoolboy-type discipline. The players also claimed that Seng Quee had embarrassed the team by walking out in the middle of a training session in front of journalists and watching fans. The players eventually voted against Seng Quee remaining as coach. In a secret vote, 13 players wanted him to go home, three wanted him to stay and one abstained. A defiant Seng Quee pressed the players to identify those who had voted for him to leave but the players, to their credit, refused to divulge the names.

It must have hurt Seng Quee who considered himself as a father figure to his players. He tried to defend himself. In a letter to Jeffrey Low which appeared in the *New Nation* on 1 December 1971, he said that the reason why he walked off the training session was because he felt that the team was training spiritlessly. For Seng Quee, discipline and complete obedience to the coach were vital.

In an interview in 1975, he revealed some of the incidences which showed that many of his players lacked discipline. He spoke of players reporting sick when they were not actually ill and players returning to their hotel rooms after the imposed curfew time.

Things came to a head in 1977. After another complaint by players of unfair treatment, he made the decision to leave his job. This came only a week after he had been congratulated by the then Singapore Prime Minister, Lee Kuan Yew, after their triumph in the Malaysia Cup.

There was also criticism that he interfered too much in the private lives of players. In one particular incident, there was the allegation that he belittled goalkeeper Lim Chiew Peng for purchasing too many household items on hire purchase. Dismissing that charge, Seng Quee retorted, *"I don't even try to control my own children, who are old enough to think for themselves"*.

Many coaches also felt uncomfortable having to work alongside Seng Quee. Over the years, the Singapore team was coached by a panel of coaches, instead of a single coach. Some were intimidated by his 'larger-than-life' character. Upon his reappointment to the coaching panel in 1976, three coaches (Trevor Hartley, Hussein Aljunied and Andrew Yap) reportedly resigned from their coaching roles. Seng Quee's reappointment had been made at the insistence of FAS Chairman, N. Ganesan. According to a newspaper report in *The Straits Times*, the three had quit because they felt that they could not work with Seng Quee as the chief coach. This was denied by FAS Chairman, N. Ganesan. Was it a case of hurt pride of the other coaches? Eventually, Trevor Hartley and Hussein Aljunied rejoined the coaching panel with Hartley acting as technical advisor.

The Visionary

Seng Quee had always sought to find ways to enhance the quality of football in Singapore. Whether it was in improving his training methods or competing against stronger opposition, he was never shy of expressing his ideas to the various football associations that he worked with.

In many ways, Seng Quee could be compared to the legendary Manchester United coach, the late Sir Matt Busby. Both were visionaries.

When the European Cup was introduced in 1955, the English Football Association decided not to send any English team for the competition fearing that it would disrupt the already packed league campaign. It was Sir Matt Busby who insisted on Manchester United taking part in the European Cup. He was convinced that playing against stronger opposition (in this case, teams from the continent) was the only way to improve his team's performance.

As was mentioned earlier, Seng Quee had always looked beyond the Malaysia Cup and set his sights on Singapore participating in regional tournaments against stronger opposition. He once said that it would have been ideal if Singapore was situated in Europe where strong opposition would be available at your doorstep.

In 1949, Seng Quee, together with some football enthusiasts, studied the possibility of creating a South-east Asia tournament while coach of the Singapore football team. His idea was to create a tournament embracing Malaya, India, Burma (now Myanmar), Thailand, Indonesia, Indo-China (now Vietnam, Laos and Cambodia), Philippines and Hong Kong.

He visited these regions (at his own cost) with the aim of talking to officials of the various bodies and seeking their views on organising such a tournament.

Sadly, the idea never materialised, though the SEAP Games (later the SEA Games) which came into existence in 1959 included football as one of the sporting events.

Seng Quee also saw youth as the future of Singapore football. That was why he proposed a juvenile football league in 1949. The league was organised with a view of spotting talent among the youngest in Singapore. A challenge trophy had been presented by W. Watt, the then President of SAFA. Eight teams registered to take part in the league: De La Salle XI, Owen Youngsters, Hotspurs, Mong Wah Football Team, Chinese Athletic Juniors, Junior Dynamos, United Brothers, and the State Express XI. The proposed juvenile league sadly never got off the ground. The Colony's education authorities made a ruling forbidding schoolboys from participating in competitions organised by SAFA.

Even up to the early 1970s, Seng Quee still harboured some ideas on schoolboy football. In a 1972 interview with journalist Jeffrey Low from the *New Nation*, he had this to say when asked about how youth football could be developed:

> "Start a soccer school, if possible, at Changi, Seletar or Tengah bases, where modern facilities are available — a dormitory to house 100 schoolboys, four soccer pitches, a gymnasium, a library, a kitchen, a store, quarters for staff (a director, qualified coaches, groundsmen, clerical staff, etc. This is a long-term plan."

This clearly sounds like the professional academies in Europe which have produced many great players.

Seng Quee was also keen on having a larger stadium that could accommodate at least 75,000 spectators. He had expressed this desire as early as the 1950s. He always cited the popularity of the Rizal Memorial Track and Field Stadium in Manila with its ability to host night matches due to the availability of floodlights, as a prime example. Back then, the largest stadium in Singapore was the Jalan Besar Stadium.

Jalan Besar Stadium

The Jalan Besar Stadium opened in December 1929. It had a capacity for 8,000 spectators. It was built to replace the Anson Stadium which hosted several Malaya Cup finals before the Second World War but could only accommodate 3,000 spectators.

The first game at the Jalan Besar Stadium took place on Boxing Day 1929 before a crowd of 7,000. It featured a game between the Malayan Chinese and Malayan Asiatic teams. The Malayan Chinese team won 3-2.

During the Japanese Occupation from 1942 to 1945, the stadium was used as a screening site during Operation Sook Ching. (Operation Sook Ching was an attempt by the Japanese army to ferret out and destroy suspected anti-Japanese elements among the Chinese population.)

In addition to hosting football, hockey and rugby matches, it also hosted community and national events like the first Singapore Youth Festival in 1955, the first Singapore Armed Forces Day in July 1969 and the National Day Parade in 1984.

The stadium hosted Malaya Cup (later Malaysia Cup) games from 1932 until 1973.

Sadly, Seng Quee's idea for a bigger stadium never materialised. It was only later at the insistence of N. Ganesan, the former Chairman of the FAS, that the National Stadium with a 55,000 capacity was built in Kallang, with the first match there taking place in 1973.

Seng Quee's vision was always way ahead of its time. In 1957, he submitted a 22-point plan to SAFA. Primary among that plan was a move to ban competitive football on Sundays in Singapore (with the exception of matches against touring teams and charity games). His view, which was shared by many players, was that players should have a break on Sunday. It would be unfair to deprive them of their only day off in the week as most of them were working people.

Seng Quee pointed out that the 'no Sunday soccer' rule was enforced in England (during the 1950s) and he saw no reason why it should not be adopted in Singapore. This move was however criticised by many including journalist Jock Bain. He argued that the average working person should be able to indulge in watching his favourite football team play on Sunday, which was his off day. The proposal was eventually not accepted by the sporting council.

In addition, Seng Quee also wanted a standardisation of all grounds used in SAFA. In his view, all grounds should be of international standard size (100–120 yards by 70–80 yards or 91.4–109.7 metres by 64–73 metres). This would have proved to be a challenge in land scarce Singapore.

Another change recommended by Seng Quee was that the duration of First Division matches be increased to 90 minutes from 60 minutes. SAFA had always advocated a 60-minute game due to the hot and humid weather in Singapore. However, Seng Quee believed that the duration should be similar to those in other countries. He wanted to ensure that Singapore was not handicapped when it competed in international competitions where a 90-minute game was the norm. He also recommended increasing the duration of Second and Third Division matches to 70 minutes.

He also recommended the exclusion of any schoolboy on the rolls of a recognised school, from signing SAFA registration papers to play for an affiliated club, though his intention was still to allow them to play for a youth club.

Seng Quee also fostered many ideas while he was national schools coach in Malaysia in 1964.

He argued that there should be a closer link-up between schools and state football affiliates and between the Football Association of Malaysia (FAM) and the Federation Schools Sports Council to create a reservoir of talent from schools to meet Malaysia's football requirements. This was part of the blueprint for raising the standard of school football drawn up by the then Prime Minister of Malaysia, Tunku Abdul Rahman.

Seng Quee's plan included creating up-to-date records of talented schoolboys which would be kept at the FAM headquarters in Kuala Lumpur so that their progress could be followed up in accordance with reports submitted by responsible teachers from various states.

Other points advocated by Seng Quee included a system of 'graduating' players from the age of eight or 10 until they leave school. This would assist young schoolboys of international promise to 'acquire' atmosphere. Also, he had a plan for taking talented schoolboy players with the national schools team on overseas trips.

Seng Quee also saw the value of allowing budding talent to watch good football. In an interview in 1949, he said that budding footballers should be given every chance of seeing the All-Indian team in action. This team, which, at that time, was ranked as one of the top teams in Asia was scheduled to play in Singapore. In Seng Quee's words,

*"It is not going to help improve the standard of local football,
if budding players, who cannot afford to pay their way into*

the stadium, are deprived of the opportunity to see really good soccer."

Seng Quee did reveal in 1978 that he had plans to write a book about his life. We do not know how far he got. Perhaps, one day in the future, his lost manuscripts might be found and a vault of wisdom would be opened and hopefully the benefactors would be the Singapore national team.

Talent spotting

For many ex-national players and fans alike, one image that sticks to their mind is that of a chubby man in a batik shirt sipping hot tea at a table at one of the many roadside hawker stalls lining Farrer Park during the 1960s and 1970s.

In addition to his role as a football coach, Seng Quee also doubled up as a football scout and he did a pretty decent job out of it. He had this innate ability to discover talent among youngsters.

Growing up in the pre-Internet era without the luxury of visual aids like video recordings meant that seeing someone in the flesh was the only way for Seng Quee to decide if a young footballer had the potential to transform from a raw diamond to a faceted gem. For Seng Quee, the advantage of living close to Farrer Park meant that he had easy access to an ever-flowing pool of talent.

Farrer Park — The hotbed of talent

It was at Farrer Park that many future national footballers were groomed (and many future stars were spotted by Seng Quee on this hallowed ground). This 9-ha plot of land which housed six football fields was the playground for many sportsmen. (In addition to football, those in track and field, tennis, rugby, hockey, swimming, boxing and squash also called Farrer Park their home.) Many kids who lived in the surrounding neighbourhoods took advantage of the sporting facilities available to them.

Farrer Park had a very interesting history. It started out as a racetrack in 1842. It was originally known as the Serangoon Road Racecourse and was run by the Singapore Sporting Club. Horse races were mostly held on weekends and attracted a largely European crowd.

Interestingly, the first aircraft landing in Singapore occurred at the racecourse in 1919 in a Vicker-Vimy flown by Captain Ross Smith.

It was renamed as the Singapore Turf Club in 1924. Horse racing remained at Farrer Park until 1933 when it moved to Bukit Timah Race Course.

Farrer Park was then opened to the public and playing fields were made available. Farrer Park was named after Roland John Farrer who was the Municipal President in Singapore from 1921 until his retirement in 1931.

Farrer Park also witnessed its share of political gatherings. In 1942, following the fall of Singapore, Indian soldiers were mustered there and urged by nationalist Subhas Chandra Bose to switch allegiance.

By the 1960s, Farrer Park had become the 'Mecca for discovering new talent'.

And it was here that Seng Quee spent long hours at the 'sarabat' (tea) stores lining the football fields sipping hot tea. His roving eyes were on the little boys running bare feet and dribbling leather balls that sometimes weighed a ton as a result of absorbing water from the frequent torrential showers.

Farrer Park was also the training ground for many of the club sides that Seng Quee had coached like Burnley United, Spider and Singapore Marble.

His training sessions were almost like a side-show which always attracted a small crowd at a patch at a corner of the pitch, sandwiched between Northumberland Road and Hampshire Road. Seng Quee would be the centre of attention yelling instructions as his charges — many with tongues hanging out and hands on hips — were going through his tough routine. Sadly, in his desire to keep the masses entertained, he sometimes resorted to unnecessary name calling of his players and making them perform almost 'circus-like' acts!

But it was at Farrer Park that many of the future legends of Singapore football were discovered.

One of them was Rahim Omar. This was what Seng Quee had to say about Rahim, *"When I first saw him at the age of 13, lanky Rahim was playing in a friendly match in the Farrer Park field. I was impressed with what I saw"*.

According to Seng Quee, *"Rahim who 'lived and slept football' was such an enthusiastic learner that at one session, he trained non-stop from 8.30am to 1.30pm. He also used to spend one or two hours learning accuracy in shooting at a target. Rahim was so good that as early as 1954, at the age of only 22 then, he had two offers from Luton Town, the Division Two English football club, to turn professional. But he didn't accept the offer because of family problems."*

Many other players like Lim Teng Sai, R. Suria Murthi, Quah Kim Song, Dollah Kassim, Terry Padmanathan, and many others were also groomed in Farrer Park by Seng Quee.

Teng Sai recalled, *"Mohd Noh and I used to walk from Jalan Tenteram to Farrer Park for our training sessions under Seng Quee when we were in our teens."*

It would have saddened Seng Quee to find out that the hallowed Farrer Park grounds and surrounding facilities will be turned into residential development. As journalist, Godfrey Robert exclaimed about Seng Quee, *"Farrer Park was his paradise, a playground where he taught and soaked in the beautiful game."*

The man with a heart

Despite his outward appearance as a strict and firm person, Seng Quee was always a man with a heart. The number of charitable acts that he performed over the years reflected the gentler side of him.

Footballers throughout the years have vouched for his generosity; whether it was providing free boots, providing bus fares for boys to come for training, paying for players' lunches and like in the case of Suria Murthi, occasionally buying 'kambing' (mutton) soup and cod liver oil!

Ex-Lions striker Ho Kwang Hock recalled, *"If we couldn't afford new boots or sportswear, he would say, 'Go and take from my shop, say Uncle sent you'."*

His acts of generosity occurred all throughout his life. In some cases, he demonstrated his generosity on a larger scale. In 1946, he proposed a charity football match for the benefit of those players who died during the Japanese Occupation. Among the players who died during the Japanese Occupation were: John Chye, Low Ah Sang and Yan Wing Fong (Chinese Athletic), Taib Senior, Taib Junior, Dolfattah, Bakri and Sheriff (Malays Football Team), Tan Lai Chuan and Chan Ah Kong (Singapore Chinese Football Association). Families of these deceased players benefitted from this charity match.

In 1949, he proposed another charity football match in aid of the families of deceased players who had rendered past services to the SCFA. As an alternative proposal, Seng Quee also suggested that one or more scholarships be instituted by the SCFA for the purpose of educating the children of the deceased players.

He also suggested a football carnival to be held in Singapore that year between Chinese representative teams from Hong Kong, Indonesia and Singapore.

In 1949, he proposed forming a Singapore Amateur Footballers' Association and one of its chief aims was to assist SAFA in looking more into the welfare of all players of affiliated clubs. Seng Quee felt that injury to players was one of the greatest problems of amateur players. *"If a player is injured during a game, he should receive free medical attention without jeopardising his amateur status,"* he argued. He further added that in a wider sense, there must be a provision for players who may suffer more serious injuries which are liable to keep them out of work for long periods of time.

During the mid-1970s, Seng Quee also fought with the FAS to increase the allowance of all players. Each player was given a training allowance of $120 a week then. During matches, there was a $10 bonus given to each player for a goal scored, $30 for two goals and $70 for three goals.

"That was why we were so motivated to thrash teams by 6-0, 7-0 score lines," said Syed Mutalib, former central defender of the Singapore team who was nicknamed 'The Gangster' for his hard tackles. *"We were not paid much but we did it all for the love of Singapore and football,"* he added.

Syed Mutalib would later respond to Seng Quee's personal generosity by opening a restaurant called House of Biryani at 96 Owen Road in Seng Quee's memory. Seng Quee's own house used to stand just a few doors away at 87A Owen Road. Sadly, the restaurant did not remain open for too long.

Seng Quee the businessman

During the 'slow' periods when Seng Quee was not at the helm of a football team or when he was not 'spotting' new talent in Farrer Park, he kept himself occupied with his sports shops business as was mentioned earlier.

It is unclear when Seng Quee commenced his sports goods business but according to Jita Singh, he already had a sports business by the early 1960s. His sports shop called Maju Jaya Sports Store was in Owen Road which was close to Farrer Park.

His shop sold all kinds of sporting goods. Many players recollect buying their first pair of football boots and jerseys from his shop.

By the end of the 1960s, his Maju Jaya Industries was doing a roaring business. They were the sole distributors of Kingswell football boots that were very popular in the 1950s and 1960s. Later in the 1970s, they also captured the sole distributorship of Diadora, the Italian sportswear manufacturer.

They were also the regional agents of Admiral Sportswear, a British sportswear designer and manufacturer. The trademark Admiral was first introduced in the mid-1960s. It gained popularity after it designed the sportswear for the England and Wales national teams and tops clubs from the 1970s like Leeds United, Manchester United and the FA Cup winners of 1976, Southampton. Demand increased not only in Singapore but also in Indonesia, Brunei, Malaysia and Thailand.

Admiral also put itself on the map in Singapore early in 1976 when it offered the FAS $1 million if the Singapore national side won the World Cup! (Singapore would make the first entry into the World Cup qualifying competition the following year.)

Piracy of Admiral products in the region became a big issue and it started eating into the healthy profits of Seng Quee's business.

At the request of his principals in the UK, Seng Quee was tasked to trace the origins of the pirated goods. He donned the cloak of a private investigator and made trips to Bangkok and Penang where he successfully uncovered the factories producing the pirated items.

In addition to his Owen Road shop, Seng Quee also later opened another shop at International Plaza.

Choo Seng Quee at a 1977 pre-World Cup qualifying game in his famous 'batik' shirt.
(Soccer Annual 1977 — Published by FAS)

Special image of Choo Seng Quee in an old football. (Designed by Edmund Aroozoo)

R. Suria Murthi beside Choo Seng Quee's grave in 2019.
(Personal photo)

R. Suria Murthi cleaning Choo Seng Quee's grave in 2019. (Personal photo)

An old map from 1900 showing Tank Road where the first football match using association rules was played in 1889.

The Singapore Chinese Football Association (SCFA) 3rd team in 1933. Choo Seng Quee is standing fourth from the left. (Malaya Tribune)

Lee Wai Tong, captain and star
soccer player of the South China
team. (Tribune).

According to N. Ganesan, former chairman of the
Football Association of Singapore (FAS), Lee Wai
Tong was Seng Quee's hero. He is often regarded
as the greatest Chinese footballer due to his
accomplishments in winning several Far Eastern
Games titles with the national team.
(Malaya Tribune)

The S.C.F.A. team which drew with the Wilts on the Padang on Tuesday.

SCFA 1st team in 1935 before a game against the Wiltshire team. Choo Seng Quee is standing first from the left. (Malaya Tribune)

Singapore's victorious Malaya Cup XI. (Tribune).

The Singapore team that won the 1937 Malaysia Cup. Choo Seng Quee is standing third from the left. The coach was 'Pop' Lim Yong Liang standing first from the left. He is considered to be one of the greatest forwards who ever played for Singapore. (Malaya Tribune)

Choo Seng Quee in 1939. He was invited to attend the preliminary selection in Hong Kong for the football team that would represent China at the 1940 Olympic Games in Helsinki, Finland. Sadly, the Games never took place due to the Second World War. (Malaya Tribune)

Victors — Singapore's Malaya Cup XI: Front Row (left to right): Hoi Meng, Tee Siang, Boon Seong, Ramian, Chye Hee; Centre: Haji Garhan, Vass, Hee Jong; Back Row: Abdul Rahman (Captain), Osman Angullia, Salleh and Seng Quee (coach of the S.A.F.A.)

The Singapore team before a Malaya Cup game against Negeri Sembilan in 1949. Choo Seng Quee was the Singapore Amateur Football Association coach and is standing on the extreme right. (Malaya Tribune)

Choo Seng Quee standing fourth from the left (and inset) with some officials of the Indonesian football team ahead of the 1951 Asian Games in New Delhi.

(Indonesian Football website — https://www.bolasport.com/read/31131767/mengenal-paman-choo-sosok-pelatih-asing-pertama-timnas-indonesia?page=all)

THE 1958 MERDEKA FOOTBALL TOURNAMENT CHAMPIONS

Standing (L to R): Kwok Kin Keng (Hon. Secretary), Lim Ah Lek (Malacca), Boey Chong Lian (Penang), Zainal Abidin (Perak), Kwong Chong Yin (Johore), Woo Ah Wah (Penang), Choo Seng Quee (Coach), Yusof Bakar (Perak), M.Joseph (N.Sembilan), E.C.Dutton (Selangor), Boey Ban Chuan (Penang), Wong Yuen Ching (Hon. Asst. Secretary).

Sitting (L to R): Ahmad Nazari (Perak), Jalil Che Din (Perak), Rahim Omar (Selangor), Chan Tuck Choy (Perak), Tunku Abdul Rahman (President), Abdul Ghani (Selangor), Lourdes (Selangor), M.Govindasamy (Selangor), Lim Kee Siong (V.President).

Sitting on ground (L to R): Mok Wai Hong (N.Sembilan), Wong Kim Seng (Perak), Robert Choe (Malacca), Ng Boon Bee (Perak).

Choo Seng Quee, standing in the back row, seventh from the left, with the victorious Malayan team that won the 1958 Merdeka Football Tournament. Tunku Abdul Rahman, the President of the Football Association of Malaysia, is seated directly in front of him. (New Straits Times; courtesy of Yuzaily Yusof)

Map showing the Farrer Park field where Choo Seng Quee nurtured many future Singapore stars. (OneMap SG)

A Sunday Nation Young Soccerites certificate awarded to nine-year-old Faizal Ashraf in 1975. The coaching clinic was conducted by Choo Seng Quee who also signed the certificate. (Faizal Ashraf)

N. Ganesan — Chairman of FAS from 1974 to 1981. He was responsible for bringing in Choo Seng Quee as the Singapore national team coach in 1977.
(Soccer Annual 1977 — Published by FAS)

Singapore supporters supporting the national team at a football
match at the National Stadium in 1977.
(Soccer Annual 1977 — Published by FAS)

The scoreboard at half-time in the final of the 1977 pre-World Cup
match between Singapore and Hong Kong at the National Stadium.
The match ended with that scoreline.
(Soccer Annual 1977 — Published by FAS)

The Singapore and Penang teams lining up before the 1977 Malaysia Cup Final. (Soccer Annual 1977 — Published by FAS)

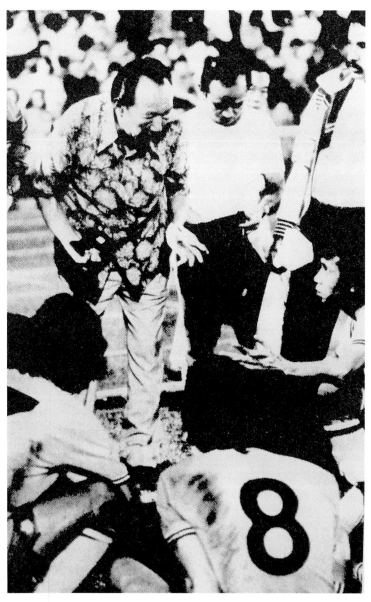

Choo Seng Quee talking to the Singapore players before extra time at the 1977 Malaysia Cup Final. (Soccer Annual 1977 — Published by FAS)

Jubilant Singapore fans after Singapore's victory in the 1977 Malaysia Cup Final.
(Soccer Annual 1977 — Published by FAS)

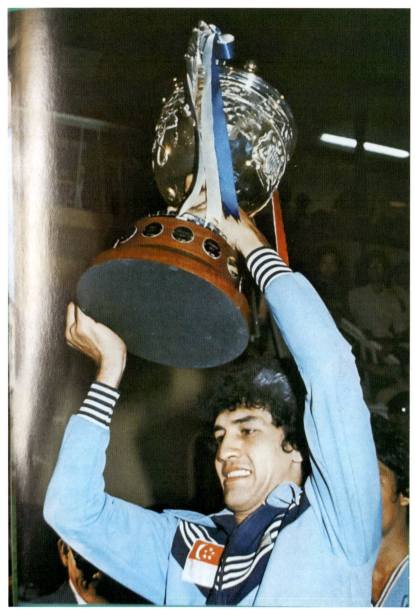

Samad Allapitchay lifting the 1977 Malaysia Cup.
(Soccer Annual 1977 — Published by FAS)

Captain Samad Allapitchay (with trophy) with teammates Robert Sim, Edmund Wee, Nasir Jalil and Hasli Ibrahim after their victory in the 1977 Malaysia Cup.
(Soccer Annual 1977 — Published by FAS)

The victorious Singapore team doing a lap of honour after winning the 1977 Malaysia Cup. (Soccer Annual 1977 — Published by FAS)

Some former national players during a discussion with the author in 2019.
From left: Robert Sim, Lim Teng Sai, Roy Krishnan, the author, Mike Seet (who helped the author get this book out) and Samsuddin Rahmat. (Personal photo)

The author (with Mike Seet) with some ex-national
football players in 2019.
Seated: Samsuddin Rahmat and Roy Krishnan.
Standing: Mike Seet, Robert Sim, Lim Teng Sai and the
author. (Personal photo)

The author and Mike Seet with former Singapore striker Quah Kim
Song (middle) in 2018. (Personal photo)

A sign showing the entrance to the Choo Seng Quee Lounge at the Jalan Besar Stadium. (Courtesy of FAS)

A poster on the wall inside the Choo Seng Quee Lounge at the Jalan Besar Stadium. (Courtesy of FAS)

Chapter Eight

The Seventies

The sixties was a decade of rapid economic growth and successful expansion of industrial activities in Singapore. It did have its fair share of challenges and major upheavals such as the policy of confrontation by Indonesia from 1963 to 1966, separation from the Federation of Malaysia in 1965, and the decision of the British, announced in 1968, to withdraw their military presence by the end of 1971.

The period of rapid economic growth with double-digit annual growth rates continued until 1973. The growth was slowed down by the world recession set off by the late 1973 massive price hikes for crude oil. But Singapore was already on its way to becoming an 'economic miracle'.

For Seng Quee, the 1970s proved to be the pivotal period in his career as a Singapore coach.

By the early 1970s, football in Singapore was facing a major crisis. The Malaya Cup victories from 1964 and 1965 were just distant memories. Singapore's fourth place finish in the 1966 Asian Games masterminded by coach Yap Boon Chuan could have been a figment of our imagination. Singapore's absence from the Malaysia Cup from 1968 to 1970 also resulted in a lack of competitive football for the city-state's budding footballers. A handful of regional tournaments provided the only form of competition for Singapore.

Singapore's record in 1970 was not one to be proud of. At the 1970 Merdeka Tournament, the Singapore team finished as wooden spoonists in their group losing all five of their matches. In the match for 11th place, the team succumbed to a four-nil defeat against South Vietnam. Hence it was six matches played, six defeats. Their only saving grace that year came in the King's Cup where they edged Hong Kong 1-0.

The alarm bells started ringing and in June 1971, the National Sports Promotion Board assigned Seng Quee once again to the national team coaching panel.

Note: The National Sports Promotion Board (NSPB), created on 1 February 1971, was a statutory body dedicated to the development and promotion of sports in Singapore. On 1 October 1973, the NSPB merged with the National Stadium Corporation to form the Singapore Sports Council.

The coaching panel for the Singapore national football team consisted of Seng Quee, Andrew Yap, Sebastian Yap and Major Abbas Abu Amin. Singapore was invited again to the 12-team Merdeka Tournament in August. Seng Quee conducted a gruelling two-week centralised training programme to prepare the team for the tournament. The players were housed at a military camp dormitory in Portsdown Road.

The tough training paid dividends. The team defeated Hong Kong 2-1 in their first group encounter. According to reporter Alex Soars, Seng Quee shed tears of joys after that hard-earned victory. A bigger shock was to come in their next match two days later, when Singapore achieved a famous 1-0 win over eventual winners and 1970 Asian Games champions Burma. This was a match where Dollah Kassim made his mark and got the vital goal through a penalty. The Singapore press dubbed this victory as the 'greatest upset in Merdeka Tournament history'.

But Singapore failed to capitalise on those impressive victories. Two draws against India and Philippines, both relatively weaker opponents, meant that they were edged out of a semi-final berth by a single point.

The NSPB kept their faith in Seng Quee and he was given the task of preparing the Singapore team for the King's Cup and the Vietnam Cup. Though the squad did not win either tournament, they received high praise from many journalists for their impressive performances.

Interestingly, for these two tournaments, Seng Quee devised two different styles of play: the Brazilian style game and the Swiss sweeper system. He felt that since the teams participating in these two tournaments would be the same as those from the Merdeka Tournament, he wanted two options to create an element of surprise!

Seng Quee stepped down from his role as Singapore coach in December 1971. According to journalist Jeffrey Low, the rumour going around was that Seng Quee stepped down because of business and health reasons.

It did not take long before Seng Quee was in the forefront again. In 1972, he was tempted back to Singapore. But he could not improve their performances in the Malaysia Cup and in the Merdeka Tournament and was allowed to leave once more.

The Singapore team embarked then embarked on a one-month long trip to the UK. Seng Quee, who did not accompany the team, did offer some philosophical advice to the players. In a letter to the *New Nation* published on 28 March 1972, he said:

> *"My advice to the national team before its departure to England is to take full advantage of the tour.*
>
> *"Take away the leaves of English soccer… take away the branches… and pull out the trunk including the roots. This is far from a pleasure trip.*
>
> *"Project a good image of Singapore. Accept strict discipline and work extremely hard.*
>
> *"Since this is a rare opportunity for all of you, do not waste your time. Learn as much as possible by asking questions. You start talking and your host will start talking. If you don't, the British won't. Talk, and there is no end."*

The rest of the early 1970s proved to be a gloomy period for Seng Quee. The Football Association of Singapore (FAS) rejected Seng Quee's application for national coach in September 1974.

He remained largely on the side-lines, grooming teenage players at Farrer Park. He kept himself occupied writing copious articles on the finer points of football for newspapers and magazines when he should have been leading the Lions.

But his golden chance came when N. Ganesan became the President of the FAS in 1976. The much-awaited invitation was made to Seng Quee to regain his much-desired position of national coach. It would prove to be a game-changing moment in Singapore's football history.

N. Ganesan

Nadesan Ganesan (or Gani as he was more affectionately known as by Singapore's football family) was the FAS Chairman from 1976 to 1981. He also doubled as the team manager of the Malaysia Cup team.

He was appointed Chairman of FAS in 1976 after serving his apprenticeship as the deputy chairman under R. B. I. Pates in 1974.

Gani was a former club footballer himself who also excelled as a table tennis player. He enjoyed sports tremendously. He was a familiar face at many sporting events, even at Inter-Constituency Games in the early 1970s.

He had a successful criminal practice. But his dedication to football especially when he became the Chairman of FAS caused his legal practice to suffer.

When he took over the reins as head honcho in FAS, one of his first objectives was to change the Malaysia Cup venue from Jalan Besar Stadium to the National Stadium. Jalan Besar Stadium had been the preferred venue for the Singapore team from the 1930s until the early 1970s.

It was a controversial move and was met with strong objections from the Council who feared that they would not be able to fill up the stadium to capacity and this would thus result in losses especially since moving from Jalan Besar Stadium to the National Stadium meant huge increases in stadium rental fees.

But Gani managed to convince the Council to see things his way. He offered to pay the National Stadium charges instead of FAS.

With the help of the Singapore Sports Council, the FAS distributed 30,000 tickets free to the schools and whipped up interest through the mass media. Gani even paid for the performances by bands at matches.

This was Gani's first plan to bring football to the grassroots. The plan worked to a tee. The crowds swelled and interest in football was revived at all levels. It was common to see crowds of up to 55,000 for most matches during Gani's tenure as FAS Chairman. That prompted the arrival of the now legendary 'Kallang Roar'.

The Kallang Roar

The Kallang Roar was born after Singapore switched their Malaysia Cup home games from the 6,000-capacity Jalan Besar Stadium to the National Stadium in 1974 — creating a 55,000-strong cauldron of noise.

What exactly was the Kallang Roar? According to one reliable source, it was Jeffrey Low, a journalist from *The Straits Times* who coined this phrase.

But though it may have been Jeffrey Low who came up with the phrase, it was Gani who was instrumental in providing the platform which allowed the 'Kallang Roar' to evolve.

In an official statement, the FAS commented that the bold and visionary move from the Jalan Besar Stadium to the National Stadium led to 55,000-strong crowds flocking to the 'Grand Old Dame' to cheer on the Lions and the various national teams, and in turn helped to create the famous 'Kallang Roar', an apt term given to the noise levels from the stands that hit a deafening decibel-measure, the echoes of which was heard from Kallang to Katong.

Former sports commentator, Wilfred James had this to say about the Kallang Roar:

> *"When I came out for my break, I heard the roar and my hair stood up. I had goose bumps on the back of my neck. I said, 'Goodness me, is this what the Kallang Roar's all about? I didn't know.'"*

Former national team striker Quah Kim Song recalled the emotions the Kallang Roar created:

"Every time when we trooped out into the National Stadium, you can get this Kallang Roar... the fans cheering us, it was full house.... That kind of feeling, I think I cannot describe."

For Gani, his gamble to host Singapore's home games at the National Stadium paid off handsomely.

"It was like a fire, you know, hoof! It went on fire. First game, (it) was 15,000 (spectators), second game 40,000, third game 55,000 and so on. For eight years, stadium was full."

Apart from the roaring success in filling up the National Stadium and overwhelming the coffers of FAS, Gani was instrumental in many other changes which elevated the status of football in Singapore.

As FAS Chairman, Gani created the blueprint for Singapore's 30-team 'super league'. Up to then, there were 118 teams in the National League. Gani hoped that by having fewer teams, there would be a greater chance that teams would be better managed and use the facilities more efficiently.

He was also instrumental in launching the Lion City Cup for players below 16 years old in 1977. It was a tournament for budding talent and was hailed as the only Under-16 football tournament in the world. It paved the way, at FIFA's request, for a World Youth U-16 tournament in China in 1985.

His other big success was arranging for the 1977 pre-World Cup tournament to be staged at the National Stadium — after a long tussle with Indonesia and Hong Kong.

Gani was fortunate to have a great committee at FAS. They worked in unison and their decisions about the development of football in Singapore were unanimous. Interestingly, in eight years as the Chairman of FAS, the only decision that was not unanimous was the appointment of Seng Quee as coach!

The resistance to Seng Quee's appointment as Singapore coach was immense. Even after Singapore's magnificent performance in the pre-World Cup competition, Gani had to fight tooth and nail again to retain Seng Quee as coach for the Malaysia Cup tournament. This as we all know proved to be a wise move as Singapore won the 1977 Malaysia Cup after a 12-year break.

What was his success formula? In an interview with Joe Dorai in 1989, Gani said:

"There is no secret formula but a deep love for the game, 100 per cent commitment, care for the players' welfare and being tough when the occasion demands it."

Gani's involvement in Singapore football during his reign as chairman was total. He had his finger in every football decision but also eventually ensured that things went his way. At times, he called for a meeting of his council members twice in a week. All because he had thought of some football idea and wanted it to be implemented.

There was no such thing as a consensus. If council members disagreed he would go at it without their backing, with an undertaking that he would take the blame.

Gani had a special ability to blend with his players but, at the same time, keeping his distance and commanding their respect.

He was awarded the Public Service Medal (Pingat Bakti Masyarakat) (coincidentally together with Choo Seng Quee) in

1978 for their big contribution towards the promotion of football in Singapore.

When he passed away in 2015, the tributes came flowing. Former Lions star Quah Kim Song said:

> *"People were sceptical over whether the stadium could be filled but Gani took the plunge. We are forever indebted to him for kick starting a golden period of Singapore football."*

Song also added:

> *"Passionate, gutsy and knowledgeable football men like him are hard to come by these days."*

To this day, stories abound of Gani's generosity. Upon learning that former national winger R. Suriamurthi had never visited India, Gani offered to cover all the expenses for his trip.

Said Suria, *"I politely declined but that showed what a man he was. He would do anything for the players."*

Lim Teng Sai, a defender in the 1977 Malaysia Cup-winning team, added: *"From hotel to food, he provided for us — out of his own pocket at times. Even if we lost, he would give us incentives and that gave us motivation to play at our best."*

Ex-national striker Fandi Ahmad said: *"He looked after me personally and always believed in my ability. I will never forget how he kept reminding me to learn from the senior players and not take anything for granted."*

An FAS spokesman described Gani as *"a larger-than-life character who left a deep mark on Singapore football"*.

Joe Dorai summed up the qualities that Gani displayed when he took football from the pits to the pinnacle:

"Total commitment, charisma, sound knowledge of the game and a reliance on the conscience even to the point of being dictatorial at times."

A national hero

On 2 September 1976, with Gani's backing, Seng Quee was brought back as chief coach of the Singapore national team. His chief task was to lead the Singapore team at the preliminary World Cup tournament held in Singapore in February 1977. This was Singapore's first attempt at trying to qualify for the prestigious World Cup. The FIFA World Cup was first held in Uruguay in 1930. The original trophy was called the Jules Rimet Trophy in honour of the Frenchman who came up with the idea of this global football tournament. After Brazil's third victory in 1970, they kept the trophy. A new trophy was created for the 1974 World Cup held in West Germany.

The decision was to appoint Seng Quee as the new Singapore coach was not a popular one. He survived a secret vote made by the council held after a stormy meeting at FAS. He succeeded by a majority of only one vote.

His unpopular appointment prompted FAS advisor Trevor Hartley, coach Hussein Aljunied and trainer Andrew Yap to resign from the coaching panel (though their resignations were disputed by FAS) although Hussein did return to assist Seng Quee in late September. Meanwhile, Hartley returned as technical advisor.

For Gani, it was important that the coach of Singapore also needed to understand the psychology and culture of the people. For him, Seng Quee was the ideal person having been in the football scene for more than 40 years. Gani only had high praise for Seng Quee. *"He is experienced, a top calibre coach and if he is ready and willing to work with us, why keep him out"*, Gani said. But, like many of his decisions, Gani also gave an assurance that should anything go wrong, he would take the rap.

For the first time, Seng Quee was able to have non-interference in the match day selection of players. This was with Gani's support.

News of Seng Quee's comeback in 1976 was greeted with jubilance from many Singapore football fans who saw him as the man to carry Singapore football forward.

But there were some insiders who bitterly opposed his comeback. Some felt that his controversial and tough methods would cause morale problems and dissension. They felt that times had changed and while the players of the older generation would tolerate his 'old school' regime, the newer generation of players would not stand for his 'archaic' ways.

But surprisingly, his first training session saw a full turnout despite rumours that some players might drop out. They were a few absentees but those who missed the session had valid reasons. Even players who were injured at that time like Samad Allapitchay, Syed Mutalib, Hasli Ibrahim and Lim Teng Sai had light workout sessions. Many of these players had been groomed by Seng Quee and were willing to undergo the almost military-like training sessions.

1978 World Cup Asia Group 1 Competition

Seng Quee's first task in his new role was to guide Singapore to World Cup qualification. He had less than six months to guide the Singapore team into uncharted waters.

The omens were not good. Seng Quee wanted the players to stay together during the preparations for the tournament. The team was forced to stay in some dormitories at the Jalan Besar Stadium. Many of the players were unhappy with the living conditions. Some said it felt like being in prison. The training regime was tough too with players having to lift weights for three hours on the day before matches.

And the friendly matches prior to the tournament did not go according to plan. The team went through a miserable run losing 4-0 to South Korea and suffering further defeats against the Russian U-23 side, Brno of Czechoslovakia and Swiss side, Neuchatel Xamax. Already fans were clamouring for his head. Seng Quee was subjected to threats via anonymous letters and telephone calls. Some went even as far as insulting his wife and children.

The successes that he had with the Indonesian and Malaysian teams seemed like a distant memory.

The odds were highly stacked against the Lions when the draw for the pre-World Cup qualifiers was carried out. With heavyweights like Malaysia, Thailand and Indonesia featured in Singapore's group, it seemed to be an arduous task. Many feared that Singapore would end up with the wooden spoon. Even South Korea team manager Oh Wan Kon observed, "*(Singapore) are not in the same class as Malaysia or Thailand*".

But, little by little, Seng Quee infused the team with a new fighting spirit and cohesive teamwork not seen in a Singapore team for many years. The team moved into a hotel to ease the tension in the camp. The centralised training which included two recalled star players — Quah Kim Song and 'Camel' S. Rajagopal — provided the right tonic to gear the players for battle and create a super-fit Singapore team. It was on Seng Quee's advice that these two players were recalled.

Kim Song, the tireless striker whose acceleration often left defenders chasing shadows, had his two-year suspension by the FAS for alleged misconduct lifted (at the insistence of Seng Quee).

Rajagopal, the 'banana kick' specialist, had decided to quit the national team after an unhappy incident with the FAS two years earlier, but was persuaded to rejoin the Singapore team.

And for the two weeks from 27 February to 12 March 1977, Singapore's 'no-hopers' played above themselves and demolished some of the best football machines in South-east Asia and debunked many myths about their lack of talent.

Seng Quee's approach to the tournament was a simple but practical one. *"The team that makes the least mistakes, takes advantage of opportunities given and rises to the occasion will win matches. It'll be the survival of the fittest,"* he said.

And what better way to kick off the tournament than a victory against a skilful Thailand team. And it was the two recalled players, Kim Song and Rajagopal, who had their names on the scoresheet. It was a perfect way for both of them to show their appreciation for the trust that Seng Quee had put in them. Lady Luck played its part too as Rajagopal's goal came off a deflected freekick. The Thais missed numerous opportunities with their exciting brand of attacking football.

At the final whistle, Seng Quee was in tears. He paid tribute to the Singapore fans cheering on their team at the stadium. *"The Kallang Roar was responsible for our win. I hope the crowd will give us the same support throughout the tournament"*, he said.

Even the Thai coach, former Thai football legend Niwat Sesawasdi, had praise for the Singapore team. *"Your players won because they had more stamina"*, Niwat conceded. It was clearly evident that Seng Quee's tough training regime was paying dividends.

However, the victory over the Thais was not sufficient to silence the sceptics who still doubted Singapore's chances especially since their next game was against the professionals from Hong Kong.

The Hong Kong team were well-prepared for the tournament. They had arrived on the back of a six-month intensive training programme and also had a budget of $150,000 provided for by the Hong Kong Football Association plus offers of attractive cash bonuses. Their Dutch coach, Frans van Balkom, had played club football in The Netherlands. He also coached Japanese outfit, Yomiuri (Tokyo Verdy), one of the most decorated clubs in the Japan Soccer League.

But the Singapore team raised their game against Hong Kong. Despite conceding two early goals, they pressed deep into the Hong Kong half. The Hong Kong team soon found themselves defending desperately against the wave of Singapore attackers. That persistence paid off and Singapore eventually forced a 2-2 draw with goals from Quah Kim Song and Dollah Kassim.

That impressive performance against Hong Kong could be attributed to Singapore's improved ability to read the game intelligently and also following Seng Quee's advice of adapting their play to each situation.

Then came the much-anticipated game against Malaysia, their perennial rivals from across the Causeway. The Malaysians then were ranked among the top four teams in the Far East. They had come to Singapore with an impressive string of trophies; among them, the King's Cup (1976), the pre-Olympic title in Indonesia in 1972, and the Merdeka Cup in 1973, 1974 and 1976.

But the Singapore team overcame the odds and defeated the fancied Malaysians 1-0 with elegant winger Mohamed Noh converting a penalty in the 32nd minute after Quah Kim Song had been floored by Malaysian defender Yahya Jusoh in the penalty box.

It was Singapore's first victory against Malaysia in an international match since 1972 when they beat their arch-rivals 3-1 in the Independence Day tournament in Saigon.

Seng Quee in his usual pragmatic self, advised his players to remain level-headed despite the victory. He told his hungry lions, *"Be humble but walk with your heads high. Don't let success get into your heads. There are still two more matches to play."* Two more matches? There was only one more group match to play but it seemed that Seng Quee was already convinced that his team would make it to the play-off final.

However, their victory against the Malaysians came at a cost. Seven players were injured. The biggest setback was losing influential midfielder M. Kumar. His ankle injury ruled him out for the rest of the tournament.

Despite losing to Indonesia in the last group match, the Singapore team secured a play-off spot.

Suddenly soccer mania hit Singapore. For the first time in a long while, there was a buzz in the air surrounding the Singapore team. One could feel the sense of excitement among Singaporeans. The recess time chatter among wide-eyed school students focussed on only one topic: the pre-World Cup final. There was a real belief that this could be the moment that Singapore could advance to the next round and become serious contenders for a place in the World Cup. Of course, stronger and more experienced opponents would come in the next round. But Seng Quee had created a team who had been conditioned both physically and mentally to believe that they could scale to greater heights.

On the eve of the final, Seng Quee was unusually calm and relaxed: The pressures that etched extra creases on his forehead before the start of the tournament had suddenly disappeared.

Speaking to reporter Percy Seneviratne before the play-off match, he said, "*We should win because my boys have still not produced their best.*" He continued, "*Their sinews will be steeled, their hearts big and strong and they will play like lions.*"

Seng Quee was confident that Singapore would win. For him the omens were also good. One morning, a few weeks before the tournament, during their customary flag raising ceremony at the Jalan Besar Stadium, a white pigeon came to rest at the top of the flagpole. When the flag was raised, the bird flew away and dropped a white feather. Seng Quee was by nature a superstitious man, so he interpreted it as a good omen. "*It was a sign from the heavens that we were going to receive good fortunes in the tournament,*" Seng Quee said.

Sadly, Lady Luck deserted them in the play-off match. Singapore lost 1-0 to Hong Kong with the winning goal coming from Lau Wing Yip. Wing Yip, at 1.6 metres, was the shortest Hong Kong player on the field.

Hence Singapore's chances of reaching the final qualifying round went up in smoke and their World Cup dream was over.

Despite the defeat, the Singapore fans stood behind their team. Several fans were interviewed after the match and many had nothing but high praise for the Singapore team. Ramamurthy Naidu, who worked as a Singapore Airlines executive said, "*Our players were just great. They gave everything but luck was not with them.*"

Another fan, Allan Han said, "*I never expected the Singapore players to put on such a superb performance. I also congratulate coach Choo Seng Quee. He has done a wonderful job.*"

There was even a young girl who called up the newspapers at 12.30am, the day after the final. Sobbing over the phone, she said, *"I want to contact coach Seng Quee. I'm still in a daze. Our team did not deserve to lose."*

A few days after the pre-World Cup, Seng Quee surprised everyone by announcing his retirement. In his words, he said that he wanted to rest and give someone else a chance to manage the team. He also said that he wanted to spend more time on his business. For a man who saw the job of coaching the Singapore national team as the ultimate honour a Singaporean could ever have, his actions cast some doubts as to the real intention of him leaving the post. The FAS under Gani made a strong plea for him to return to his coaching role.

There was also a series of public appeals including an open letter from journalist Jeffrey Low. In his open letter, Low called Seng Quee, *"the Messiah of Singapore football"*. In the conclusion of his letter, Low had this to say:

> *"But if you still feel that you ought to retire from coaching now because of your age and business, let it be known that the name Choo Seng Quee will be as legendary to Singapore soccer as Pele is to world soccer."*

In Seng Quee's reply to Jeffrey Low's open letter, he wrote that he had a funny dream. In his dream, a huge figure in white robe appeared before him, with the background no other than the National Stadium. He then added that thousands and thousands of fans were giving a tremendous ovation. The huge figure then said to him, *"You must continue with your good work. You and your boys will receive my blessings!"*

He eventually agreed to stay on as national coach on a voluntary basis with performance-based payouts.

He then paid tribute to Gani for backing him up as well as thanking his assistant coaches, Hussein Aljunied, Majid Ariff, Rahim Omar and Andrew Yap. "*Soccer is in my blood. As such I want to be involved again in coaching — at any level,*" he declared.

Victory in the 1977 Malaysia Cup

A book on Choo Seng Quee would not be complete without talking about the 1977 Malaysia Cup. In the eyes of many Singaporeans, this was his most famous victory. We have already touched on it briefly in the earlier part of this book.

Why do many people today fondly remember that victory in the 1977 Malaysia Cup? For a start, it meant the end of a 12-year drought that had seen the Malaysia Cup safely remain in the peninsula. By some strange football quirk, Singapore until 1977 just could not win the Malaysia Cup. For seven years (1968 to 1974), they could not even make it to the final. The Lions then reached the final in 1975 and 1976 but were tamed on both occasions by their 'bête noire', Selangor.

The 1977 Malaysia Cup campaign saw a Singapore team in full confidence. Seng Quee's 'boys' powered their way to the final with an unbeaten record. In the preliminaries, Singapore finished as South Zone champion with a tally of 18 points, scoring a massive 35 goals and conceding only six.

Singapore's results in the South zone:

Beat Malaysian Armed Forces	7-1 (home)
Beat Negri Sembilan	2-0 (home)
Beat Malacca	6-0 (home)

Drew with Trengganu	1-1 (away)
Drew with Johor	0-0 (away)
Beat Malacca	3-0 (away)
Beat Trengganu	4-3 (home)
Beat Johor	6-1 (home)
Beat Negri Sembilan	3-0 (away)
Beat Malaysian Armed Forces	3-0 (away)

The semi-final saw them once again pitted with their arch-rivals, Selangor. Selangor had always been the 'bogey' team for Singapore. They had lost the previous two finals to their fierce rivals.

The Singapore team edged Selangor 2-1 in the home leg at the National Stadium, thus preserving their record of never losing at home to Selangor since 1973.

However, many were convinced that Singapore would not be able to overcome Selangor in the return leg at the Merdeka Stadium. Many Singapore players had a phobia against playing in the Merdeka Stadium where the crowds were aggressively hostile. And the host team were frequently openly out to maim the Singapore players.

Also, the Selangor fans came in full force for the second leg. Many Singapore players on the bench were on the receiving end of plastic beer glasses, golf balls and other missiles thrown by many of the 40,000 Selangor fans. Even Seng Quee was himself hit.

But the Singapore team overcame their phobia in away matches and ran out 2-1 winners thus winning the semi-final tie 4-2 on aggregate. The man of the match was most certainly goalkeeper, Edmund Wee. Edmund, who was playing for the first time at the Merdeka Stadium, saved three almost certain goals from efforts by Selangor danger man Mokhtar Dahari and captain Soh Chin Aun.

It was off to another final but this time against Penang, their rivals from the north. The previous occasion, these two teams had met in the final, the headline in *The Sunday Times* of 14 September 1958 screamed: "*Malaya Cup goes to Penang as Singapore fail in replay.*" In the losing team of that 1958 final were two Quah brothers, Kim Swee and Kim Beng. Their younger brother, Kim Song, would now try to make amends and secure victory for the Singapore team.

The match was played at the Merdeka Stadium again, though Penang had earlier requested for the final to be transferred to their home ground, The City Stadium.

The Merdeka Stadium was filled to the brim for the final. Though the admission prices were higher than in previous years, all the tickets were snapped up. There were also many Singaporeans who watched the final on television. It was estimated that over 900,000 adults (aged 15 and above) tuned in to the live telecast.

The pitch was damp and soggy due to the incessant rain before the match.

The final started off brightly for Singapore who took a 4th minute lead through the 'mercurial speed demon' Quah Kim Song. He received a cross from S. Rajagopal who manoeuvred past Penang defender Annuar Osman, and scored with a diving header.

However, we all know that all it takes is for one incident to turn a game on its head, and sadly that happened against Singapore's favour in the 29th minute. A feeble back pass by Singapore captain Samad Alapitchay to goalkeeper Edmund Wee was neatly intercepted by the quick-footed Penang striker Isa Bakar and he calmly put the ball past a helpless Edmund. The aftermath of that goal saw defenders Syed Mutalib and Hasli Ibrahim having a verbal exchange with skipper Samad. Seng Quee sensed that something was not right.

After that goal, Singapore seemed to disintegrate. Its passes became wayward. Everything seemed to go wrong. The tide seemed to have turned against the Singapore team. And the Penang team which up to the equaliser had not been playing great football by any reckoning, was effectively sending long balls into the Singapore half, which almost always landed at a Penang foot.

After being on the offensive while Singapore retreated further back into their lines, Penang deservingly took the lead in the 35th minute. It came off a corner and in the ensuing scramble, Ali Bakar, the older brother of Isa, pounced on the loose ball and slotted the ball into the net.

By half-time, Penang was clearly the dominant team and seemed destined to score more goals in the second half and hence carry the Malaysia Cup back to Pulau Pinang as they had done so only three years before.

Was it going to be third time unlucky for the Singapore team, having lost the Malaysia Cup final the two previous years? Was it going to be another year of disappointment for the 6,000 travelling fans cheering on the Singapore team at the Merdeka Stadium? Or for the many thousands glued to their television sets at home or in the community centres back in Singapore?

The Singapore changing room at half-time was dead silent. One could almost hear a pin drop. Eighteen players in the light blue colours of the Singapore team huddled close to each other in the stadium changing room with sullen looks and eyes staring hopelessly at the mud-stained floor. Their jerseys were drenched and muddy as a result of the incessant rain that refused to secede. There were no FAS officials in the changing room at Seng Quee's request.

For Seng Quee, dressed in his usual 'batik' shirt, it was almost 'déjà vu'. He had faced a similar situation 12 years before in 1965 when his Singapore team were a goal down but came back to score three goals in the final 17 minutes to defeat the mighty Selangor team 3-1.

In his cool and calm manner, Seng Quee simply said, "*Samad, I'm taking you out. Teng Sai, you are coming on*". All the players looked stunned. He was replacing their captain and 'rock' of the team with a young novice. But Seng Quee had sensed that Samad was not playing his usual game. Was it cup final nerves or something else? In a post-match interview, Seng Quee justified his bold move to replace his captain, "*Yes, it was a bold move which not many coaches would not dare to make. But Samad could not recover from the mistake and was not playing his best. So I had to replace him to prevent more quarrels on the field.*"

Young Lim Teng Sai would prove his doubters wrong and turned out to be an able replacement.

Singapore's midfield dynamo, V. Khanisen, had also put in a below par performance during the first half. Seng Quee had instructed him to shadow Penang centre-forward Isa Bakar which he did. But that prevented him from displaying his usual midfield creativity. During the interval, he pleaded with Seng Quee to allow him to play his normal game. Seng Quee agreed and it was only in the second half that Khanisen showed up.

According to former national player Quah Kim Song, Seng Quee also gave the players a crucial pep talk. Kim Song said, "*Uncle Choo then told us that we had not won the Malaysia Cup for 12 years and that he had prepared us thoroughly for the match and also studied our opponents, the Penang team, in detail. He said he strongly believed we could win in the second half, despite being 1-2 down.*"

Seng Quee was in tears when he spoke to his players. (Brian Richmond, who was commentating for the final, passed by the dressing room during the half-time break and saw Seng Quee in tears. Seng Quee confessed to him that he was putting on an act!)

But that act was sufficient to galvanise Singapore in the second half. Seng Quee's magic seemed to be working.

The gutsy Singaporeans showed the '*semangat*' ('spirit' in Malay) pledged to coach Seng Quee earlier. Seng Quee, a great psychologist with football teams, had conditioned his players into an invincible frame of mind where sticks and stones from the Malaysian fans could not shake. Their mental strength started to show.

Their pressure paid off when Singapore equalised in the 71st minute through 'super-sub' Nasir Jalil, nicknamed 'The Crazy Horse' for his abundant energy and perpetual motion on the field. It was lucky no. 13 for Singapore as Nasir Jalil wore a no. 13 shirt. 'The Crazy Horse' had come on for the disappointing 'Camel' S. Rajagopal, whose 'banana kick' in swinging corners caused mayhem to opposing defences in the matches leading to the final. Perhaps the big occasion proved to be too much for 'The Camel'.

Towards the end of the game, tensions mounted and reached boiling point. Yellow cards were flashed at hard men Syed Mutalib and N. Baskaran by Malaysian FIFA referee Koh Guan Kiat for some questionable tackles.

The energy levels of both teams descended south and safety-first became the name of the game as both teams seemed more concerned with not conceding a goal rather than going on the offensive. The game thus meandered into a lull as the game ended in a deadlock and went into extra time.

The Penang team were especially feeling the effects of the gruelling struggle. Seng Quee's gruelling training regime for his Singapore boys seemed to be paying dividends.

And Seng Quee was confident that his team would win. The first thing he told his players when he walked onto the pitch during the short break before extra time was that they were going to win the match.

His exact words were: *"We'll win this game, go get the goals."*

But it was still touch and go during the 30-minute extra period. But one golden chance fell to Singapore.

The Singapore team was awarded a free kick in the Penang half. The 'gelek-king' Dollah Kassim then delivered a perfect cross and Kim Song, in typical fashion, dived and nodded the ball past goalkeeper Rahim Mohammed in the 105th minute. The two had practised this move on numerous occasions on the training ground and their telepathic communication proved vital.

Penang pressed on in the second half of extra time with midfield ace Shukor Salleh prodding the Bakar brothers forward in search of the elusive equaliser.

And with the clock winding down, a chorus of 'Que Sera Sera' could be heard coming from the brave Singapore fans who had endured the taunting from the hostile Malaysian fans at the Merdeka Stadium.

Then, like music to the Singapore fans ears, the referee blew the final whistle.

The teams on that day were as follows:

Singapore: Edmund Wee, Hasli Ibrahim, Syed Mutalib, Samad Allapitchay (Lim Teng Sai), Robert Sim, Zainal

Abideen, V. Khanisen, Mohammed Noh, Quah Kim Song, Dollah Kassim, S. Rajagopal (Nasir Jalil).

Penang: Rahim Mohammed, Anuar Osman, Ooi Hock Kheng (Nik Hassan), Lim Cheng Hock, N. Baskaran, Shukor Salleh, Radzi Ahmad, Fadzil Ismail (Gopalkrishnan), Isa Bakar, Ali Bakar, Ravi Varma.

Referee: Koh Guan Kiat (Selangor)

The Malaysia Cup was heading back to Singapore after 12 long and frustrating years. Seng Quee had achieved what other coaches had tried and failed to achieve since 1965, the year of Singapore's separation from Malaysia.

An emotional wave swept the nation as jubilant Singaporeans celebrated the victory. It was a proud day to be a Singaporean.

Seng Quee proved his worth in this final. The final demonstrated the thoroughness of the old maestro's skill in getting the best out of his boys. He made those tough decisions to replace his captain, Samad Allapitchay, and the fans' favourite, S. Rajagopal. Not many coaches would have been prepared to take a gamble of replacing such key players and incurring the wrath of the fans had things not gone the right way. But Seng Quee displayed the courage that had seen him overcome tough challenges throughout his coaching career.

Quah Kim Song, in an interview several days after their famous victory said that Seng Quee had helped him cool his nerves before the game. "*Uncle (Seng Quee) was certainly the calmest person around and we could not have made it had it not been for him. Such was his strength and he transmitted it to us to the extent that we could have played for another full hour.*"

The Malaysian press also had high praise for the Singapore team and Seng Quee. Reporter, George Das of the *New Straits Times*, had this to say of Seng Quee: "*The one motto he (Seng Quee) has drummed into them is that non-fighters are losers, and they proudly displayed this fighting spirit by coming back from the brink of defeat to snatch the Cup from Penang's grasp.*"

George's colleague in the *New Straits Times*, Png Hong Kwang, also praised Seng Quee for developing the super fitness in the Singapore side.

Many said that this was the pinnacle of Seng Quee's career and in many senses rightly so since the Malaysia Cup had eluded Singapore for 12 long and painful years.

Seng Quee had succeeded in helping his players overcome their 'Merdeka Stadium hoodoo'. Using his great psychological abilities, he conditioned the Singapore players into an invincible frame of mind which sticks and stones from Malaysian fans could not shake.

For many of the Singapore fans (even though about 7,800 tickets were allotted to Singapore fans, there were many other Singapore fans who bought tickets in the open market) who crossed the Causeway to watch the final, it was a night to remember. Many of them braved the terrible treatment dished out by the Malaysian supporters. Sadly, some of them were not there during the victory celebrations after the final whistle blew. According to well-known Singaporean blogger, 'Unk Dicko', his wife's cousin, together with several other fans, were arrested by the Malaysian police during the match. Their crime: shouting 'Referee *kayu*' (a fan insult directed at a referee for making incorrect decisions in a match) too loudly. They were taken to the police station and only released the day after!

The victory celebrations continued on at the Holiday Inn in Kuala Lumpur. In an interview in 2003, the late Dollah Kassim had this to say when asked about the atmosphere at the hotel: *"Wah, electrifying is the first word I can say. I don't know what word to use, after the finals when we won the game, you should have seen the celebrations. The jubilation from the Singapore crowd was fantastic. We could hardly go into our hotel in KL. It was so crowded."*

For Seng Quee who was a firm believer of the 'old school of thought' — going to bed early, no smoking or drinking before tournaments etc. — the lavish celebrations were out of character. Some 200 fans were there at the hotel lobby to witness the great coach drink champagne out of the Malaysia Cup! The more fortunate saw him smoking a cigar and staying up the whole night on that special evening.

With tears flowing from his eyes, he paid homage to the Singapore fans who had stood thick and thin with the team, braving the objects and insults thrown at them by the Malaysian fans.

Seng Quee always had a way with words that at times bordered on Shakespeare! But at other times, the words that flowed from his mouth could be brutal and many players have wept after a torrent of expletives. We shall leave this side of Seng Quee to the imagination.

When asked by journalist Jeffrey Low what his emotions were just after the final whistle at the Merdeka Stadium, he said:

"I had a date with 'Miss' Malaysia Cup. I asked her if she would like to come back with me to Singapore. At first she was reluctant, saying that she left our country for 12 years because we did not take good care of her.

"Even after 90 minutes of coaxing and persuasion, she was still stubborn. But I told her that my family (the players) and I will show her how determined we are to win her heart.

"Finally, after another 30 minutes, she was convinced. And we won her heart and soul. Yet she still had a condition for me. She said she go back next year if I am not there.

"So I had to promise her that even if I do not have the chance to show my family how to take good care of her, the family and the future families will prove to her that they will be as dedicated as ever.

"And her final words were: 'I will try it out for one year. If you can pass the test again, I will willingly stay in your country for as long as possible.' I then told her that God will be with us to help keep the promise."

Many Singapore fans greeted the victorious Singapore team at the Paya Lebar Airport. Several of the players were lifted shoulder high by delighted airport workers.

There was speculation that a victory parade would be held in Singapore to honour the victorious Singapore team. To everyone's disappointment, no victory parade was held. FAS Chairman Ganesan said that such a venture would not be possible. *"We have to think about security, traffic and general crowd behaviour"*, Gani said. Furthermore, he felt that such a parade would blow the victory completely out of proportion. He reiterated that it was a moment *"for objectivity and humility."*

The victory in the Malaysia Cup in 1977 was greeted with joy from all quarters. Edmund William Barker, the then Singapore National Olympic Council (SNOC) Chairman and Minister for Law and the Environment, made two promises to the team (and kept them) if they won the Malaysia Cup: He hosted a dinner for them at the Istana and got the Prime Minister of Singapore at that time, Lee Kuan Yew, to grace the occasion. E. W. Barker had known Seng Quee as early as 1932 when he was his junior in Raffles Institution. He said that Seng Quee's interest in football was then already out of the ordinary.

For the dinner at the Istana, Lee Kuan Yew surprised everyone by walking in — in his golf attire.

For Seng Quee, it was a great honour to meet Lee Kuan Yew, someone he had always held in high esteem. At the dinner, Seng Quee recited proudly to Lee Kuan Yew the words "Untuk Bangsa dan Negara" or "For Nation and Country", which he constantly mouthed to his boys to take pride in their homeland and play for the national flag.

Offer and gifts came in from all directions from jubilant Singaporeans. Over $6,000 worth of gold lighters were presented to FAS by Texton Asia Limited for the Singapore team as a reward for winning the Malaysia Cup. The representative for Texton said that the gesture was in tribute to the tremendous spirit and determination of coach Choo Seng Quee and his boys for winning the cup.

Honoured at last

On 9 August 1978, Choo Seng Quee was awarded the Pingat Bakti Masyarakat (Public Service Medal). It came 29 years after his first stint as coach of the Singapore national team. His beloved nation finally recognised his hard work and dedication to elevating the status of football in Singapore. The credible second place in the pre-World Cup competition and victory in the Malaysia Cup proved to be catalysts for his well-deserved award.

At the interview after he received his PBM, Seng Quee said:

"It is indeed a rare honour after being involved in football promotion for more than 40 years. The year 1978 will be the most memorable one of my life. First I had the rare honour of meeting our Prime Minister, the second was when I was selected as coach of the year, and now national recognition. I wish Singapore and Singapore soccer well and I will continue to contribute in any way I can."

Joe Dorai, a former *Straits Times* sports reporter who closely followed Seng Quee's exploits for almost 15 years said that the award to Seng Quee was well deserved for the sacrifices and dedication that he had made to help Singapore achieve football success.

Lost momentum

The Singapore national team under Seng Quee looked unbeatable. The focus was now on the 1977 SEA Games which was to be held in November 1977. Sadly for Singapore football, a sudden turn of events halted the momentum generated by the victory in the 1977 Malaysia Cup. On 27 June 1977, Seng Quee announced that he was resigning as coach. He had rejected a one-year contract offer by the FAS. Many were bewildered by his sudden decision to resign. The talk along the corridors centred on the unhappiness of the players over the disparity in bonuses and mistreatment by the management. This led to an alleged boycott of training.

Seng Quee was also getting fed up with the personal threats against him. Before the Malaysia Cup semi-final second leg with Selangor, he received numerous telephone calls threatening him with bodily injury should he travel with the team to Selangor. He had also received threatening letters enclosed with defaced copies of his photographs. The telephone calls according to Seng Quee were received by his daughter at his sports shop in Owen Road. But strangely, such threats did not seem to bother him. He did not report them to the police, and dismissed them as the work of pranksters or from gamblers who lost money after Singapore's victory in the first leg.

However, his wife, Margaret Boon Khin Siang and his three children — son Boon Keng, Robert and daughters Geok Lan, Theresa and Geok Kim, Helen — took those threats seriously. They had been persuading him to give up coaching since the pre-World Cup tournament in 1977 and with the latest string of threats they made renewed attempts to get him to retire. But those pleas fell on deaf ears and Seng Quee trudged on.

So while his decision to resign after the 1977 Malaysia Cup was greeted with disbelief by the nation, his wife, Margaret, was in fact thrilled with his decision to resign. She had been his closest confidante and stood by him throughout his football career as a player and as a coach.

In an interview with the *New Nation* which was reported on 26 June 1977, a beaming Margaret had this to say, *"It is better for him to give up. They do not appreciate what he has done."*

She further validated his dedication to the Singapore team by adding, *"He is old now, and his health is not so good. Can you imagine what it is like for him to stay up well after midnight, thinking of training methods? And he keeps to himself so much, always thinking of how to improve Singapore football."*

Sadly for Margaret but to the joy of thousands of Singapore fans, Seng Quee withdrew his resignation after talks with the FAS and the national players.

Preparations for the SEA Games resumed but then the unthinkable happened. Seng Quee had accidentally cut his right foot with a razor during the World Cup qualifiers. Typically being his stubborn self, he ignored the wound, preferring to concentrate on Singapore's continued rise towards the summit of South-east Asian football. Unfortunately for Seng Quee, the wound turned septic. He said, "*The thrills and excitement of big tournaments numb pain. And it's only after everything is over that you feel it once again.*"

The infection worsened after a fall in the dressing room at the Merdeka Stadium during a Malaysia Cup semi-final against Selangor in May 1977. But Seng Quee's mind was still focussed on victory in the Malaysia Cup.

Lim Teng Sai, a 1977 Malaysia Cup-winning defender, said, "*The only time we ever saw his swollen leg was when he showed it to a player who was not running for the ball. (Seng Quee told the player) 'If I can walk around with a leg like this, I don't see why you can't run with your limbs both in good order.'*"

By September 1977, gangrene had set in on Choo's wound. A decision was made to have his right leg amputated to the knee. Surgery was performed on 12 November. It proved to be a tricky operation given his diabetic condition. As a result of spreading gangrene, a further amputation on his right upper leg was performed five days later. On his hospital bed, Seng Quee's heart stopped three times — during the first and second operations, and a third following internal bleeding. It must have been a tormenting moment in his life. He was forced to spend three months in the hospital.

Following his operation, the FAS decided to relieve Seng Quee of his duties as national coach on medical grounds. Seng Quee though was adamant about continuing coaching. "*Though I've lost a leg, I've not lost my head, enthusiasm and spirit,*" he said. He even released a set of photos showing his rehabilitation to the press, hoping to prove his fitness to return as Singapore coach.

Seng Quee admitted that he regretted not keeping fit. Football had always taken priority over his health. Dr. Bill Fung, head of the FAS medical panel, had reminded Seng Quee on numerous occasions to watch his health but his pleas fell on deaf ears.

Even after the amputations, Seng Quee was determined to make a comeback and coach the Singapore team. In an interview with journalist Joe Dorai immediately after his discharge from hospital in early 1978, Seng Quee pledged to return to coaching as soon as possible. He was determined to continue coaching even if it meant coaching from his home. However, the FAS had other ideas. They were determined not to recall him on medical grounds.

There was also the issue of Seng Quee's refusal to have an artificial leg fitted. Two businessmen, one from Indonesia and the other from Malaysia, had offered to take Seng Quee to the then West Germany to have an artificial leg fitted. But Seng Quee refused the offer stating that the time was not right for him to travel especially long distances.

Seng Quee's idea on the other hand was to use players who had trained under him to assist him in his training sessions. They were to be the ones to demonstrate any tactics and actions that needed to be carried out. Sadly, this was not within FAS's scheme of things.

Seng Quee's days as a football coach seemed to be numbered. The Singapore coaching role for the SEA Games tournament was handed over to Hussein Aljunied. Singapore performed dismally in the 1977 SEA Games. The team still comprised many of the same players who had excelled in the pre-World Cup and Malaysia Cup tournaments only a few months before. But they were held to a draw by a weak Philippines team before losing to both Thailand and Burma. Was it a case of being too complacent after their earlier successes?

When asked for his opinion about Singapore's performance, Seng Quee replied, "*I could not bear to watch them play in the SEA Games. They were awful. I switched off my (television) set.*"

Some journalists were also in favour of Seng Quee returning to coaching. They urged the FAS to reconsider bringing Seng Quee back as coach. As one journalist pointed out, "*Uncle Choo, although confined to the wheelchair at the moment, is still the best man around, and we contend that a one-legged Seng Quee is still far more capable than the many physically able coaches that we have at the moment*".

But, in spite of his absence from the football field, Seng Quee was never far from the news. He was highly critical of the Singapore team's performance during the 1978 season. He even took a dig at some of the journalists who were covering the football scene in Singapore. One journalist later remarked that Seng Quee seemed to be blaming FAS for his misfortunes (of losing his limb). He urged Seng Quee to stop the sour grapes attitude.

Seng Quee approached the FAS several times to offer his services but each time the FAS held back and relied on Dr. Bill Fung's advice that he was not fit to return to football.

While Seng Quee faced a brick wall in Singapore, there were other teams outside of Singapore keen on securing Seng Quee's services.

In 1980, a firm offer came from the Johore Football Association to coach their team. The Malaysia Cup season was already halfway through but Seng Quee pounced at the opportunity. This was the opportunity he had been waiting for.

The Johore team had not been performing well despite having a forward line which consisted of one former international (Hussein Mohammed) and three current 'B' internationals. However, under

Seng Quee's guidance, the team started to 'click' and became strong contenders to reach the semi-finals of the Malaysia Cup. The highlight of the season though was the clash between Singapore and Johore at the Larkin Stadium.

It pitted Seng Quee against Jita Singh, who was once coached by Seng Quee in the early 1970s. Jita, who had taken over the Singapore team, had proven his mettle by leading Singapore to impressive performances at the pre-Olympics, the SEA Games and the Thai King's Cup.

It also set Seng Quee against many of his former protégées. Two-thirds of the Singapore team were made up of players who had trained under the 'old master': players like R. Suria Murthi, Samad Allapitchay, Mohammad Noh and Edmund Wee who had benefitted from Seng Quee's wisdom.

The pre-match preparations were marred by allegations against Seng Quee's loyalty to Singapore. According to journalist Suresh Nair, Seng Quee was upset that "*some people*" were branding him as disloyal to Singapore just because he became part-time advisor to the Johore soccer team. Seng Quee lamented, "*What have I done to deserve this kind of treatment? Why are these people being unkind to me?*"

Seng Quee was also disturbed by news reports which he felt questioned the allegiance of some of his former protégées like Mohammad Noh, R. Suria Murthi and Edmund Wee. "*I've never encouraged any player to play against his country.*"

The match between Singapore and Johore ended in a 2-2 draw which, in the end, was a fair result, considering that the Singapore team had to put up with a hostile crowd and an almost grassless pitch. Though Seng Quee must have been disappointed with the result, he must have been glad to see his protégée, Mohammad Noh, grab both of the Singapore goals.

The Johore team finished seventh in the 1980 season, winning seven and drawing four matches out of the 16 matches. They missed out on a semi-final berth by a mere three points. The future looked promising for the Johore team. Seng Quee knew that if he was with the team from the start rather than coming on board mid-season, the team's prospects would be brighter.

Sadly, on 7 January 1981, Seng Quee surprised everyone by announcing his retirement from football with a shocking statement which included, *"I hate football!"* In an interview with journalist Suresh Nair, he added, *"Please don't talk football to me. I had a strange dream a few days ago. A big figure appeared before me and told me to give up."*

He further added, *"I am firm about it. There'll be no U-turns. I intend to be more spiritual and to learn more about the teachings of God."*

He ended the interview with his now familiar lament: *"I've been ignored. Nobody, it seems, wants to benefit from my 40 years' soccer experience. Everything I've learnt will be buried with me."*

The Johore FA said that they would attempt to get Seng Quee to change his mind. Many expected this to be one of his usual tantrums. To the detriment of football, there was no turning back this time.

Seng Quee's stint with Johore was to be his last hurrah in football. Apart from his usual rantings in the press about the Singapore team's performance in the Malaysia Cup, he kept a low profile, though any call from FAS or any other team would have seen him eagerly heading back to the football frontline

But Seng Quee's absence from the limelight did not stop others from recognising his contributions to football. In 1982, the Indonesian Football Federation awarded him a First Class Gold Medal in appreciation for his services to Indonesian football. The presentation was made by Soepariyo Ponce Winoto, Chairman of the PSSI, at Seng Quee's residence in Thomson Road.

Chapter Nine

The Last Days

On 30 June 1983, Seng Quee died at his home in Wolskel Road. He was 68. A few weeks before his death, Seng Quee was hospitalised in Mount Elizabeth Hospital with a recurring kidney problem. But he asked to be discharged from the hospital a day before his death so that he could be united with his wife and his three children.

The tributes poured in from many in the local football fraternity. Jita Singh who was the current Singapore coach then said, *"We've lost a great coach"*. He added that Seng Quee was instrumental in putting Singapore soccer on the Asian map in the 1960s and early 1970s.

The Chairman of the Football Association of Singapore, Teo Chong Tee, who was also the Parliamentary Secretary (Social Affairs and Environment), paid tribute to Seng Quee and added, *"He will always be remembered as one of the greatest local soccer figures this century."*

Ex-Singapore goalkeeper Edmund Wee, who had become a professional player and was playing in Hong Kong, highlighted Seng Quee's paternal instincts. *"He was like a father to me. He gave me very good advice before I left for Hong Kong. I owe my success as a professional solely to him."*

Another former Singapore player, Robert Sim, also remembered Seng Quee's paternal instincts. He recalled an incident when

Edmund Wee was ill during a football tour and Seng Quee had brought fruits to him in the latter's hotel room. He told Edmund, *"Mesti makan buah-buahan (Must eat fruits)."*

Other tributes flowed in. Lee Kok Leong, who was once rated by FIFA as one of the 12 best referees in Asia, was saddened by Seng Quee's passing. He lamented, *"Singapore has lost another Grand Old Man of Singapore Soccer".* He added, *"Uncle's string of successes would go down in the record books as one of the best achievements by any sporting personality this century. We've indeed lost a great soccer gentleman."*

Other former national players like Ibrahim Awang and Quah Kim Beng expressed their gratitude for what Seng Quee had done. Kim Beng remembered his time when he was being coached by Seng Quee at Star Soccerites. *"We will never forget him for what he has done for us. Some of his actions may seem harsh at the time when we were young but now when we have grown older, we have come to appreciate his good sound advice,"* Kim Beng said.

Perhaps, sports journalist Ken Jalleh summed up the man in the most exquisite manner. He said, *"Choo Seng Quee will be remembered for more than just soccer. He will remain the finest symbol of the Singapore sportsman; unassuming, humble, who fights for what he believes is right, and knows how to take victory as well as defeat, praise as well as criticism. We do not have many more men of his breed left in Singapore sport."*

More than 1,500 fans attended his funeral wake and around 500 mourners were present at his burial. Among the men who carried his coffin were his only son, Robert Choo, his daughter's fiancé, Steven Yap, and his 'football' sons — R. Suria Murthi, Ho Kwang Hock, Edmund Wee, Quah Kim Song, and Terry Pathmanathan.

Chapter Ten

His Legacy

It has been almost 40 years since Choo Seng Quee left this earth. For many, he is now just a distant memory; a mere statistic among a list of people who have coached the Singapore national team. But for many older ardent Singapore football fans, his is a name that evokes memories of another era where the term 'soccer craze' wasn't about football from a distant land but one from our own shores. This was a man who dedicated almost 40 years of his life to football — even when he had become wheelchair-bound after losing his limbs to diabetes. To the end, he kept his voice ever-present in the local football scene, urging his wisdom on young coaches and players.

Choo Seng Quee will be remembered in many ways. Shortly after his death in 1983, a writer using the name, 'J. Singh' wrote to the *Singapore Monitor* (an afternoon newspaper in Singapore in the 1980s) requesting the Football Association of Singapore (FAS) to study the possibility of staging a tournament in which teams from Singapore, Malaysia and Indonesia (in particular those Choo Seng Quee had coached) would compete for a 'Choo Seng Quee' Cup.

The idea was that in holding such a tournament, which could be an annual affair, we would be able to show our deep appreciation for the late Choo Seng Quee. The tournament, in the writer's view, would commemorate the memory of the late Choo Seng Quee who had spent most of his life in the interests of football in the region. *"What better way to honour Uncle Choo,"* the writer added. Sadly, nothing came out of this rather interesting proposal.

However, a special match in memory of the late Choo Seng Quee did take place on 30 December 1983. It was between the Singapore ex-internationals and Malaysia ex-internationals. The Malaysian team included M. Chandran, their great ex-captain. Chandran was once coached by Uncle Choo. Playing in that match was also Singapore football legend Fandi Ahmad. Fandi held Seng Quee in high esteem. Even though he was never under the respected coach's tutelage, he consulted Uncle Choo before joining Indonesian club Niac Mitra in 1982.

Journalist Jeffrey Low summed up Seng Quee's wonderful life in an article just after Seng Quee's death. In his words:

"Seng Quee never gave up on football — a career he had dedicated over 40 years of his life to. Seng Quee was the last of a dying breed. By the time he retired, football had moved on from the fifties, sixties and seventies. His successors with the team, Sebastian Yap and later Jita Singh applied modern methods to football coaching.

"Perhaps his death, as often happened, allowed for some perspective. Whatever his flaws, Seng Quee could now be seen for what he was, a figure of immense importance in the development of football in South-east Asia. Not just for what he did for Indonesia, Malaysia and Singapore, but for what he did to the game as a whole. He was a man of principle who loved the game more than anything else. As a coach, he will always rank among the best.

"Most of all however, Seng Quee was respected for his age and knowledge. Those who came under his charge wanted to oblige him like a son would a father.

"It is possible to see a man who won the hearts of more than one nation as well as a host of trophies, who helped shape some great teams at country and club level, who warrants a place in history he has been denied for too long.

"He dedicated everything to football, to spreading the word, and sacrificed everything for it too. Seng Quee could have created a great Singapore team had he been given an opportunity."

How Choo Seng Quee fares with other Singapore national coaches

Since Choo Seng Quee's death in 1983, many people have tried making comparisons between local and foreign coaches who have coached the Singapore team.

Joe Dorai, the late *Straits Times* journalist, may be one person who may be able to place Seng Quee's position among all the other coaches having interviewed and tracked Seng Quee's movements since the mid-1960s. However, as Dorai correctly pointed out, making comparisons is always a tough job especially when comparing football coaches. It is rare to find two coaches with the same ability, character or match-winning methods although their qualifications may be similar.

Dorai also highlighted that comparisons are subjective, in much the same way as arguing who is the better footballer, Pele or Maradona. The debate can go on till the cows come home.

But there could be certain relevant facts which can help determine who the better coach is, especially in sports like football, where the coach's ability is gauged by results, players' attitude and motivation.

How would Seng Quee fare when compared with the other coaches who have coached the Singapore national team?

Since its independence in 1965, Singapore has had numerous coaches both local and foreign who have endeavoured to create a team capable of matching the best in South-east Asia and in turn Asia.

The foreign coaches included Lozan Korcev (1967–1968), Mike Walker (1972–1974), Trevor Hartley (1976–1980), Milous Kvacek (1992), Ken Worden (1994), Douglas Moore (1994–1995), Barry Whitbread (1995–1998), Jan Poulsen (2000–2003), Radojko Avramovic (2003–2012), Bernd Stange (2013–2016), Tatsuma Yoshida (2019–2021) and Takayuki Nishigaya (2022–).

The local coaches included Yap Boon Chuan (1966–1971), Ibrahim Awang (1974), Hussein Aljunied (1975–1977, 1984–1986), Sebastian Yap (1977–1978), Jita Singh (1979–1984, 1989), Seak Poh Leong (1987–1988), Robin Chan (1990–1992), P. N. Sivaji (1992–1993), Vincent Subramaniam (1998–2000), V. Sundramoorthy (2013, 2016–2018), Fandi Ahmad (2018) and Nazri Nasir (2019, 2022).

If we were to measure success by the number of silverwares won, then the trophy table would be as follows:

1. Choo Seng Quee
   - Ho Ho Cup, 1965, 1967
   - Malaya Cup, 1965, 1966
   - Malaysia Cup, 1977
2. Radojko Avramovic
   - Tiger Cup (now known as the ASEAN Football Federation (AFF) Championship), 2004, 2007, 2012

3. Douglas Moore
   - Malaysia League, 1994
   - Malaysia Cup, 1994
4. Barry Whitbread
   - Tiger Cup, 1998
5. Jita Singh
   - Malaysia Cup, 1980
   - Ovaltine Cup Tournament, 1982
   - Tsingtao Cup Quadrangular Tournament, 1983

Hence, if silverware was the criterion, then Seng Quee's name would be higher up in the ladder, especially if you were to also consider his achievements with the Indonesian and Malaysian teams. However, trophies alone may not truly reflect the quality of a coach.

In an interview with former Singapore coach Jita Singh, he said, *"Each coach will have his strengths and weaknesses. We also need to consider other factors like the quality of the players you have as well as that of the opposition, the environment and the era that you were playing in."*

For Seng Quee, two out of the five trophies that he won were in the Ho Ho Cup. (The Ho Ho Cup was first presented in 1924 by the Ho Ho Biscuit Factory in Singapore and played between Malayan/ Malaysian and Hong Kong Chinese teams. The Malaya [later Malaysia] squad could include Singaporean players until 1969. Starting from 1970 onwards, all teams involved were permitted to insert several non-Chinese players. Up until the early 1970s, the Hong Kong team was the 'Combined Chinese' team, whereby any Chinese player based in Hong Kong was eligible to play for the team, regardless of his affiliation to either the Hong Kong Football Association or the Chinese Taipei Football Association.)

Hence, Seng Quee was actually coaching a Malaysian Chinese team which comprised several Singapore Chinese players. It was only in 1975 that the tournament was played as a triangular tournament with Singapore Chinese as the third participating team.

In addition, would victory in the Malaysia Cup be considered as a greater achievement than a fourth place finish in the Asian Games (as achieved by Yap Boon Chuan with the Singapore team in 1966)?

How about the achievement in the 1980 pre-Olympics qualifications by Singapore under Jita Singh where Singapore finished above China and North Korea?

Or what about qualification for the third round of the World Cup qualifiers (as was the case with Radojko Avramovic in 2010)?

Thus if silverware cannot be used as a yardstick for a coach's greatness, what other criteria could be used? Perhaps there isn't any. Each coach was successful (or sometimes unsuccessful) in his own way. Seng Quee sprang from a generation where old school values like discipline and not confronting your elders prevailed.

When Jita Singh took charge in 1979, he inherited most of Seng Quee's experienced players. Jita's selection had come after he led the Singapore Intermediate team to the final of the King's Cup in 1978.

It was not an easy task for Jita as he had to cope with players who found it difficult to respect him as much as Seng Quee, since many had played with him when he was a player. But he managed to overcome the problem with tact and motivation.

N. Ganesan, the former FAS Chairman, was mainly responsible for the development of Jita as a high-quality coach. Ganesan arranged for Jita to be sent to West Germany and England for coaching courses and attachments with European clubs.

Jita steered the Singapore team to the 1979 pre-Olympic group final after historic victories over China, North Korea and

India. They lost to Iran in the final. He also captured the Malaysia Cup in 1980.

Jita's success with the Singapore team landed him the Coach of the Year Award from the Singapore National Olympic Council in 1980 (the only other person to win this prestigious award was Seng Quee).

In addition, Jita's other achievements included a silver medal for Singapore in the 12th SEA Games in 1983 and a runners-up spot in the Merlion Cup tournament in 1983.

Jita had a shrewd football mind. Like Seng Quee, he also adopted lots of psychology to motivate his players.

When comparing Jita and Seng Quee, discipline is a common factor.

In Jita's opinion, Seng Quee was more focussed on the individuals first and then the team. For Jita, the Dutch 'Total Football' philosophy from the 1970s completely changed the emphasis to more playing as a unit than focussing on the individual. This could perhaps explain why many football fans can remember individual players from the earlier days by name and would find it difficult to remember any of the players donning national colours in recent years!

Seng Quee was a great advocate of attacking football. But his strategy varied with the opposition, according to Jita.

For Joe Dorai, Seng Quee was in another league. Dorai, who made a comparison of Seng Quee with four other local coaches — Sebastian Yap (1978), Jita Singh (1978–1981), Hussein Aljunied (1984–1986) and Seak Poh Leong (1987–1988), was convinced that, in terms of achievement, none of those coaches could match Seng Quee who was voted the 1977 Coach of the Year for regaining the Malaysia Cup after a 12-year drought.

What made Seng Quee an outstanding coach, he said, was his ability to get the best out of his charges. *"Seng Quee had the knack of knowing the exact ability of the player and extracting it from him. Sometimes Uncle Choo also made the player give extra. He could make rebellious players — such as Quah Kim Swee, Lee Kok Seng, Matthew Chin and S. Rajagopal — slog for his cause."*

But Joe Dorai also saw the darker side of things. He said that several times he saw players go down on their knees and sob because of his verbal abuse. Most players were afraid of being publicly abused by Seng Quee and to avoid embarrassment, they worked hard to please him even though he punished their bodies.

Another comparison was made by journalist Jeffrey Low in his pre-match report before the Malaysia Cup game between Singapore (coached by Jita Singh) and Johor (coached by Seng Quee) in 1980. Back then, man for man, Singapore, according to Low, had the better players. But Low referred to Seng Quee as a brilliant tactician who was *"capable of transforming likely defeat to victory with dressing room dressing down, both at halftime and before kick-off."* Though Jita was riding on the back of some impressive recent performances in the pre-Olympics, SEA Games and the Thai King's Cup, he did admit that Seng Quee at that point of time was still the master coach in the region. The game ended in a 2-2 draw thus preserving the honour of both coaches.

Former Singapore captain Thambiah Pathmanathan summed up the different coaches this way:

"Coaches have their own characters and own ways of dealing with players and preparations. All of them want to do well.

"To say who is the best is difficult. But based on results and development of players, Seng Quee appears the best we have had."

Chapter Eleven

Uncle's Own Words

In his long and chequered career both as a player and as a coach, Seng Quee was never shy of expressing himself in words and in writing. He was a favourite among journalists looking to fill up the spaces allocated to them in their newspaper articles.

He was so eager to contribute that leading newspapers in Singapore like *The Straits Times* and *New Nation* regularly invited him to write weekly columns for their eager readers. By the late 1940s, his words and opinions appeared frequently in the daily fare for the masses. A complete book could have been written of his words of 'wisdom'.

Here is a small compilation of some of his wise words over the years:

> *"Always make the ball do the work. Always remember, the ball is your slave."*

Singapore Free Press, 23 January 1954.

> *"My basic condition as a coach is 100 percent co-operation from all the players."*

The Straits Times, 25 July 1957.

"Soccer is a young man's game. In youth the eyes have fantastic swiftness, limbs are marvellously supple, with powers of resilience and recovery.

"My plan is to build up the youths instead of relying on players who are past their best.

"They must be willing to sacrifice anything and everything for football... to practise and master all the skills, otherwise it will be of little use. There is no substitute for skill."

The Straits Times, 21 May 1959.

"My loyalty is with Singapore and there is no better way that I can prove it than by coaching the football team."

The Straits Times, 23 June 1966. These words were said when he was allegedly offered a recall back to coach the national team in 1966 (though this recall offer was refuted by the then FAS President, Awang Bakar Pawangchee).

"A coach can never bestow upon the players — no matter how young the talent under his instruction — the ability to play football.

"Although you can teach soccer, there is a limit to what tuition and practice can do. One must be born with natural skill."

Choo Seng Quee who believed that a soccer coach was not a teacher but a supervisor.

"Besides knowing soccer in all its details, the coach must also have plenty of goodwill and be well-informed of the latest developments in the game. The coach must also know the styles of all teams until it is almost impossible for the opposition to confuse him with an unknown plan of attack or defence."

In an interview given to Lim Tiong Wah of the *New Nation* in 1971.

"Many people had the wrong idea of the purpose of coaching — and that included some intelligent and knowledgeable people inside the game."

New Nation, 3 August 1971.

"My advice to the national team before its departure to England is to take full advantage of the tour. Take away the leaves of English soccer... take away the branches.... and pull out the trunk including the roots. This is far from a pleasure trip. Project a good image of Singapore. Accept strict discipline and work extremely hard.

"Since this is a rare opportunity for all of you, do not waste your time. Learn as much as possible by asking questions. You start talking and your hosts will start talking. If you don't, the British won't. Talk and there is no end. One month is too short. You cannot learn much if you are mute. You can only learn by asking questions. The more, the better."

Advice to the Singapore team before they left on their tour of England in 1972.

"If you can collect a few from each, it is worth the trip. Take them to the field to demonstrate their skills and secrets. I am sure they will oblige if you ask for it. They learn their trade secrets as early as eight or 10 years old. By 15, an up-and-coming English player is almost ready for professional soccer. It is a big business."

New Nation, 29 March 1972. Speaking to journalist Jeffrey Low just before the Singapore team went on a one-month trip to the UK.

"Don't talk seriously about professional football now. Talk about raising the standards of our players first. There are so many footballers here who have not even mastered basic skills.

"To do that, you must have knowledgeable coaches. But do we have such local coaches? Maybe I'm a coach, that's why I always emphasise the subject. It's the biggest problem.

"Soccer crowds are not fools. They are choosy. And they don't want to see bad football even if it is professional football. Without crowds to a stadium, the game dies a natural death.

"How do we convince the present players that professional football can work in Singapore by the end of next year? Firstly, they must be highly paid. But name me one footballer now who deserves to be highly paid?

"Most of our players are also suspicious of the long-term benefits of professional football. We must have expertise — from administrators to players. That means you have to spend money. Think big and act big.

"Professional football is the survival of the fittest, of those with self-discipline, and it is going to be tough for us to make this venture in the near future — not at least until after 1975.

"When I said last week that I might accept a professional coaching job in Hong Kong, I was thinking of Singapore. When I return after a year, I will have a good knowledge of the modern professional set-up, and will be ready to join the rest.

"We can do it in a small way first — like introducing non-amateurs who must have their own clubs and grounds to train. But whatever the plans are, bear in mind that incentives rule world football."

New Nation, 9 July 1973. Seng Quee's response when the view had been advanced that professional football might provide the ballast to raise the standard of football in Singapore.

"When you build a house, there must be a proportionate mixture of sand and cement. You can have the best materials but too much sand could mean the collapse of the house."

The Straits Times, 3 September 1976. Speaking to journalist Percy Seneviratne. He said this to the national team with the hope of trying to instil national consciousness into the Singapore team.

"I was a forgotten man. But now I'm a public figure. I don't want money. Neither do I want status. I only want respect."

The Straits Times, 15 May 1977. He said this when there was talk that he would be made Director of Coaches after Singapore's excellent performance in the 1977 pre-World Cup competition.

"Public memory is short. They cheer you today and jeer tomorrow."

This was what many players remember Seng Quee saying on many occasions.

"Singapore players should let the ball do the work for them because my theory has always been that a player can never be fitter than the ball. And the ball can never get tired."

Seng Quee on the 1977 Malaysia Cup final.

Majid Ariff — *"How long does it take to become a star?"*
Choo Seng Quee — *"If you are prepared to train very, very hard — one year."*

Former Singapore football legend posing a question to Seng Quee when Majid was a 19-year-old.

"Nothing in this life is free. You have to work for something to be successful, even as footballers. You have to make sacrifices."

Lawyer and academic Faizal Ashraf remembered hearing Choo Seng Quee saying this to a group of children at the Sunday Nation Young Soccerites soccer camp in 1975. Faizal, who was then nine years old, also remembered seeing his father's former student, national footballer S. Rajagopal ('The Camel') at this soccer camp.

Choo Seng Quee's tips on cup final football

This was his advice to the Singapore team on the day of the 1975 Malaysia Cup final between Singapore and Selangor.

"We do not want players who hold back when there's a 50-50 chance they may lose the ball in a tackle. There are those who are tip-top when the going is good, but cannot be relied upon when the going is hard.

"Singapore must keep their cool and not lose their heads, however irritated they are by bad sportsmanship involving players and spectators. You should ignore abuses by the spectators. If possible, plug cotton wool in your ears. This calm and collected composure must be kept throughout the game.

"Playing possession football to tire the opposition is good. But when the opportunity offers itself, a move or two must be accelerated to push the ball quickly to the front line instead of running with the ball.

"All top teams are prepared to concede midfield to the opponents. It is goals that count, and goals win matches. Goals are not scored in midfield, but in and around the penalty area. To challenge in midfield would be foolish. But shooting space must be defended at all costs.

"Defenders are knit more closely on the edge of the penalty area than on the half-way line. Defenders must try and seal off all angles of passing.

"The square pass is a time waster, and should only be used to change direction of attack. Full backs can thrust forward but the twin stoppers at centre-back should not be encouraged to attack. Midfield players must be encouraged to push the ball forward quickly. Make it simple, make it quick.

"In organising a counter-attack from midfield, players must be aware that time is of vital importance. In 10 seconds it should be possible to have all 10 players of the attacking team back in defensive positions — no matter where they are when the move breaks down.

"We should concentrate 75 percent of our efforts on scoring goals, more goals than the opposition.

"One last point: I cannot over-stress the importance of individual expression, outside the general pattern of play to a player's confidence. For it is much easier to destroy than construct. Therefore, attack must be superior to defence."

Chapter Twelve

His 'Sons' Speak

Sometimes as authors, we tend to reinterpret the words of our interviewees according to the style that we deem fit for publication.

However, in this chapter, I have decided to allow the words to flow directly from the mouths of those whose lives have been touched by the genius of Choo Seng Quee. I have attempted to minimise the amount of editing in the interviews with people whose lives were touched by Uncle Choo so that their voices could be heard in its purest form.

The words of his football 'sons' (and the people who knew him well)

"Seng Quee was a dedicated coach, and one of the best in Asia. He could have managed a British First Division team if given the chance. He was a unique coach because of his love for the game. He understood the game. He studied the game. He had a book with lots of sketches of goals scored even from as early as the 1920's. He was a football thinker. He knew how to train his team. He knew the coaching methods. He also had the attitude to discover players, to spot talent."

N. Ganesan, Chairman of the Football Association of Singapore (FAS) from 1976 to 1981 in an interview with National Archives dated 3 July 2008.

"A giant of a man in the pages of Singapore soccer history."

Joe Dorai, *The Straits Times* journalist who wrote about Choo Seng Quee from 1962 to 1983. He said this in an article in *The Straits Times*, 25 December 1977.

"Uncle has been a slave to soccer since the first day he played at the Anson Road Stadium."

Rahim Omar, Singapore soccer legend from the 1950s and 1960s speaking to journalists in 1961 after Choo Seng Quee was sent to the UK in 1961.

"Choo Seng Quee is the grandfather of Singapore football."

Teng Kim, *The Straits Times* journalist who interviewed Choo Seng Quee and the article which appeared in the *New Nation* on 25 January 1975.

"Let's face it, there are no local coaches who are as good a strategist or tactician as Seng Quee."

Justin Morais, coach of Tampines Rovers in 1976 when asked whether the decision to appoint Seng Quee as the national coach was the right one.

"Seng Quee had the knack of knowing the exact ability of the player and extract it from him. Sometimes, Uncle Choo also made the player give extra. Besides, he had a sharp eye for raw talent and the right method to nurture the youngster into top-class material. He was the best all-round Singapore coach."

Dollah Kassim (in 1979), Singapore national team player from 1969 to 1979. Affectionately known to local football fans as 'The Gelek King'.

"He's one of the best coaches we ever had. A man who knows the game well."

Lim Tien Jit (Rocky), Singapore national footballer from 1970 to 1979.

"Uncle Choo always said, Eurasians are good and stylish goalkeepers."

Brian De Rozario in an interview with Peter Rodrigues reported in the *New Eurasian*, July–September 2010.

"Choo Seng Quee is a man who believes that there is always something to learn about soccer and is always eager to learn something new."

Charlie Chan, President of the Star Soccerites, the club founded by Seng Quee (who later became a member of the FAS and the national team manager).

"A good coach should know about tactics. Not only does he concentrate on sharpening the players' skills, he must think in terms of team build-up. Uncle has got that quality."

Ibrahim Awang, former midfield hero of Singapore in the 1960s speaking to *New Nation* journalist Sonny Yap in 1975.

"He (Choo Seng Quee) taught me the finer points of soccer, ball control and the art of shooting."

Leong Hoi Meng, considered one of Singapore's fastest forwards of the 1950s speaking to *New Nation* journalist Sonny Yap in 1975.

"Seng Quee is in a class by himself. I strongly believe if Seng Quee was in England, he would be wanted by many professional clubs as a coach. Comparing their methods and his, I think he has a wider knowledge, covering continental methods as well as those used in other countries."

Peter Corthine, who had trained as a youth under Arthur Rowe, the English coach who introduced the 'push and run' system with Tottenham Hotspur, an English First Division team in the 1950s. Peter Corthine eventually went on to play for Chelsea football club and even played alongside Jimmy Greaves (who lies fifth on the list of England's all-time leading goalscorers — behind Harry Kane, Wayne Rooney, Sir Bobby Charlton and Gary Lineker). His brother, Jackie played for Spurs. In 1957, Peter joined the British Services and was stationed in Singapore. He played in the Services football team and had the opportunity to train with Seng Quee. So impressed was he with Seng Quee's training methods that he travelled four times a week from Nee Soon to Farrer Park (a lengthy distance in the 1950s) just to train under Seng Quee. In his words, Seng Quee was the best coach he ever had in Singapore and even in the UK.

"Sincerely I don't think I have ever come across a man more enthusiastic in the game. He trains hundreds of youths now but gets nothing in return but the satisfaction of seeing them play good soccer."

Peter Corthine.

"Apart from having a sound knowledge of the game, Choo Seng Quee is wholeheartedly interested in soccer. He is a staunch advocate of clean soccer."

Singapore Amateur Football Association on appointing Choo Seng Quee to coach the Singapore team in 1949.

"Choo Seng Quee was a first-class strategist. I respect him highly and I (still) consider him one of the best coaches in the region."

Lee Kok Seng, Singapore's longest serving captain who played in seven Malaya Cup finals, including the 1965 Cup final when Seng Quee was the coach of the Singapore team.

"Uncle was a very good planner and first-class strategist. The team had full confidence in him. He is the one man I know who can write volumes on the game."

Freddy Chew, former national left-back from the 1960s and 1970s.

"Choo Seng Quee was a very dedicated coach."

Chia Boon Leong (also known as 'Twinkletoes'), Singapore footballer from the 1930s and 1940s.

"Choo Seng Quee was a soccer genius who boasted that anyone who trained with him would make it to the national side."

Brian Richmond, well-known disc jockey in Singapore who also represented the Singapore national football team in the late 1960s.

"Uncle Choo's tactical play was excellent. He not only talked to us but also gave demonstrations. And his execution of skills was so accurate I was astonished. At tournaments, it was his habit to stay most of the time in the dressing room of the Merdeka Stadium and not in the posh hotels provide for foreign coaches. He felt that to understand the boys, he should be with them. Even after training, he would talk soccer to us. This man is so absorbed in soccer he knows more about the game than anyone else in the region."

Ungku Ismail, Johor team player who was coached by Choo Seng Quee in 1980.

"Thank you, Seng Quee!"

Lee Kuan Yew, former Prime Minister of Singapore when meeting Seng Quee at a reception after the Singapore team had won the 1977 Malaysia Cup.

"Choo Seng Quee was a very strict and demanding coach. Players were fearful of him. But that fear made them train harder and give 110%."

Seak Poh Leong, former Singapore team captain from 1973 to 1976. He remembers Seng Quee training the Star Soccerites team at Farrer Park. Then at 16, he started training with Farrer Park United and through the recommendation of his coach, Uncle Paul, Poh Leong had two training sessions with Uncle Choo.

"He's a strict disciplinarian, no fooling around. 'Eat football, sleep football, talk football'."

Samad Allapitchay, former captain of the Singapore national team from 1977 to 1981.

"Seng Quee emphasised team unity by making the players sing the National anthem the first thing in the morning. We had to sing loud and clear. The captain would raise the flagpole at the Jalan Besar Stadium. At the end of our singing, Seng Quee would shout out, 'Untuk bangsa dan negara, satu, dua, tiga (For the nation and country, one, two, three)', and we would have to shout out, 'Majulah (Onward)!'"

Robert Sim, tough former left-back of the Singapore team who played under Seng Quee during the 1970s. By the early 1970s, the hallmark of Seng Quee's training sessions was the recital of the National Anthem. He remembers the centralised training sessions in the early 1970s.

"I owe it to Uncle Choo for all my footballing talent. He spotted me at 12, and made me juggle with the ball for two hours every day. He also provided me with equipment from his Maju Jaya sports shop, and occasionally bought me 'kambing' (mutton) soup and cod liver oil."

R. Suria Murthi played for Singapore from 1977 to 1991 and also played for Pahang in the Malaysia Cup, and is the proud owner of the record for playing the most number of Malaysian clubs in the 1990s.

"You could hear when Uncle was coming. He always had lots of coins in his pocket. He used the coins to discuss football tactics."

R. Suria Murthi.

"He was never lacking in ideas and techniques. He followed closely the latest developments in the game. If you did something wrong, his habit was to pester you until you learned to do it right.

"All of us who went through him still admire him. Look at the stars he brought up — Leong Hoi Meng, Ho Hin Weng, Foo Hee Jong, Lim Eng Siang, Yip Chong Kam, Chye Hee, Quah Kim Beng."

Jimmy Tan, former national left-winger who represented Singapore in the 1950s speaking to *The Straits Times* reporter Sonny Yap in 1975.

"Seng Quee was the one who groomed me in my early days. I learned a lot from him. He knows everything about football and I respect him."

Rahim Omar speaking to journalist Florence Lim in 1975.

"He was respected sometimes beyond logic, sometimes beyond toleration, sometimes even beyond one's self-respect. But, in the end, his 'sons' never questioned the biggest lesson he taught them: To die for the country.

"But having no peers in soccer coaching was not enough for Uncle. He wanted to be an educationist, moralist, wicked sergeant-major, preacher, singer, orator, leader, cry-baby, fighter and philanthropist all rolled in one.

"It was impossible for him to chase such a dream. But geniuses are sometimes blind to these earthly truths. So Uncle never varied till his dying day.

"A true perfectionist believes in only the best."

Jeffrey Low, journalist who wrote a beautiful epitaph after Choo Seng Quee's death.

"In an attempt to make me hungry to score goals, Choo Seng Quee once told me to sleep with a football."

Roy Krishnan, former Singapore winger who was once rated as the best winger in Asia.

"You remember Uncle Choo Seng Quee, the former coach of the Singapore soccer team? Well, you can call me the Choo Seng Quee of the SIA team. Uncle Choo was deeply concerned about the well-being and cooperative spirit of his whole team, from the captain downwards. So am I. Uncle Choo gave short shrift to those who violated the team spirit. So will I, whether he be a manager or a worker. Uncle Choo was tough. So am I. Uncle Choo could blow his top. So can I."

Devan Nair, then National Trades Union Congress President and industrial relations trouble-shooter during a speech to members of SATU (Singapore Air Transport-Workers' Union) on 4 April 1981. Devan Nair, who later became the President of the Republic of Singapore, was responding to clashes between rival factions who were contesting for the leadership positions in SATU.

"Uncle Choo was very strict. No laksa, no rojak and a list of other types of food (that I can't remember) that he prohibited us from eating. He was a disciplinarian and helped shape our values. We trained every Saturday and Sunday from 3–6pm at the old Farrer Park field rain or shine — 90 mins ball skills and another 60–90 mins of two-sided games. Then he gave money to a boy to buy drinks from the 'sarabat' store for all the 20 odd teenagers. He provided many balls and dribbling sticks, and more importantly his time, passion and love to develop the young ones. He was known to scold vulgarities at players but I never heard him utter vulgarity at us teenagers. I trained under him for slightly more than a year before he joined the national team. Our loss was the Lions' trophy. He offered us discounts at his sports shop at Owen Road but we couldn't even afford to buy decent sportswear. Most of the time, I could only do 'window shopping' at his shop and to say hi to my beloved Uncle Choo."

Edmund Wong, who, as a teenager, trained under Seng Quee along with around 20 other teenagers from 1975 to 1976. The team had no name. The idea, according to Edmund, was for Seng Quee to keep the boys off the streets.

Eric Paine on Choo Seng Quee's training methods

In an oral interview given to the National Archives of Singapore, Eric Paine, Singapore's former goalkeeper from the early 1970s, described Seng Quee's training methods:

"Choo Seng Quee advocated physical fitness. He told us that to be able to play good football, you must enjoy the game. And if you are not fit, you will suffer. And if you suffer, you cannot enjoy the game. But the amazing thing is that he does not pile everything on you at one go. Old as he was, his physical build-up is progressive. And at the end of the training programme just before a tournament, we were able to do the following:

1. *50 thirty metre sprints*
2. *Weight training — circuit training of 10 stations (3 rounds — 10 stations)*
3. *Drinking hot teh 'o'*
4. *Running up and down the National Stadium steps 50 times*
5. *Line up at the National Stadium and do 40 laps (16km)*
6. *Last three clear all the equipment.*
   Afternoon (4–7pm) — ball play, tactical play
   His reading of the opponents play was phenomenal."

Eric remembers the Singapore team watching the Hong Kong team play against Indonesia in the pre-World Cup tournament in 1977 where the Indonesian team lost 0-3. Eric remembers the Hong Kong team who were a professional team then and described their play against Indonesia as a knife slicing through butter.

Seng Quee analysed their play. For the next three days before the Singapore–Hong Kong game, the focus was on how to counter the tactics of the Hong Kong team. According to Eric, the Hong Kong team played directly from defence to attack with the forwards shielding the ball and laying it off for the oncoming midfielders. Hence, the drill for the defenders for the three days before the game was just to head the ball away.

In addition, Eric was also asked to do sprints to meet the oncoming midfielders.

Seng Quee also noticed that the Hong Kong wingers were excellent dribblers. Hence, the task for the defenders was to deliver 'crunching' tackles.

Majid Ariff's view of Choo Seng Quee's training methods

In an oral interview given to the National Archives of Singapore, Majid Ariff, Singapore's football legend who represented the Asian All Stars in the 1960s, spoke highly of Choo Seng Quee:

> *"In 1957 someone spotted me training by myself and informed Choo Seng Quee. I met Seng Quee and asked him how long it would take for me to train to be able to play for Singapore. He said, 'Train every day for one year come rain or shine.' Seng Quee even offered to pay me a monthly wage so that I did not have to work. (Majid said that Choo Seng Quee offered to pay him around 70 or 80 dollars a month.) Training started at 7am. Dribbling around sticks until 10am. And then again from 4–6pm. I was pre-warned about Choo Seng Quee's character and fierce temper. So psychologically I was prepared. He had a fierce temper but he had a kind heart. Then it was throwing the ball in the air and stopping it with any part of the body. Ball control with the head. (Majid practised until he could control the ball with his head 200 times.) Then it was practising my dribbling skills. Uncle Choo was not satisfied with my first performance even though I thought I did well. He wanted me to improve myself even more."*

Interview with Quah Kim Song

This interview was conducted via a questionnaire that I had sent to Quah Kim Song on 17 January 2018.

RP — Reynold Pereira

QKS — Quah Kim Song

RP: You mentioned that you first met Choo Seng Quee when you were 15. What were your first impressions of him?

QKS: I had been warned by my brothers who had been coached by him — Kim Beng, Kim Choon, Kim Swee, Kim Siak and Kim Lye — that he was a strict disciplinarian, a no-nonsense guy. I was thus apprehensive and afraid. When I met him, he was larger than life, standing 6 foot 2 with a reputation that was hard to match, because he had been national coach of Malaysia and Indonesia before that, and achieved success with those teams.

RP: When he did his personal sessions with you and Jaafar Yaacob, what was the routine like?

QKS: His routine was very structured. He knew what he was going through with us:

    (1) Ball control with the outside foot;
    (2) Dribbling between poles whilst keeping possession of the ball;
    (3) Shooting at goal from 25 m to 30 m distance;
    (4) Heading;
    (5) Ball control from h0, chest, thighs and feet.

We did this as drills, repetitively, in order for us to play effectively in a game, as these were necessary skills for a football game.

RP: You mentioned that he did not get on well with the Administrators at the Football Association of Singapore. Are you aware of any personal encounters he had with FAS which were not pleasant?

QKS: All I knew was that he was not recognised by some of the administrators, as he had a reputation of wanting to manage the team his way without interference from the officials.

RP: It is said that Seng Quee played a major part in getting your suspension lifted. What were your emotions when you realised what he had done for you in this situation?

QKS: Of course, I was excited and happy that I could play and be coached by him. I am sure that he and Ganesan would have faced opposition from the other officials as I had only served three months of my two-year suspension then. I really did not believe that the suspension could be lifted.

RP: You mentioned that some of his training methods may not have been correct if you compare them to today's training methods. Can you give some examples?

QKS: Uncle Choo's knowledge of football as a coach is encyclopaedic, as he reads extensively and does his research from other countries like England. We were put through some weight training which he said was necessary as he left we needed strength to play. However, some of the detailed implementation may not be approved today.

One example was we carried weights on our shoulders and had to squat all the way down and come up repeatedly; that could have injured our ankles and knees. Another example was, he gave us hot tea during breaks so that we would not gulp down the drinks and hence not be too heavy. However, today's wisdom is to hydrate as much as possible during the game.

RP: You mentioned that he used psychological warfare games to toughen your minds and bodies. Can you give some examples?

QKS: After the group briefing, he would go to us one-on-one to re-emphasise each player's strengths and give confidence to us individually. He would fire us up individually by highlighting the critical role each of us was to play to bring the team success.

RP: How did you feel when Seng Quee made the players sing the national anthem before each training session?

QKS: I felt this was very good. It made us feel patriotic that we were playing for the country. When we sang perfunctorily, he would get upset and make us re-sing until he was satisfied that we were singing from our hearts. That, I believe, gave us 10 to 15 percent more on the field.

RP: When you were in the changing room at half-time in the Malaysia Cup final in 1977, did Seng Quee say anything to motivate the players for the second half (besides replacing Samad with Teng Sai)?

QKS: First of all, Uncle Choo did not allow any officials into the dressing room as he was going to make a crucial change, to replace the captain. We were shocked at the decision to replace Samad with Teng Sai. Uncle Choo then told us that we had not won the Malaysia Cup for 12 years and that he had prepared us thoroughly for the match and also studied our opponents, the Penang team, in detail.

He said he strongly believed we could win in the second half, despite being 1-2 down.

RP: How would you compare Seng Quee with the other coaches that you have worked with?

QKS: For me, it is simple. He could get the best out of me when he coached me. The other coaches gave us the same training programme for the whole team. Uncle Choo gave me personalised tips like asking me to practise weaving in and out, which I could do as I was short and had a low centre of gravity.

Special interview with Cheng Ding An

Cheng Ding An is the director of the Singapore hit movie 'Kallang Roar the Movie' which centred around Choo Seng Quee and the Singapore 1977 Malaysia Cup winning squad. This interview was conducted via a questionnaire that I had sent to Ding An on 19 December 2019.

RP — Reynold Pereira

CDA — Cheng Ding An

RP: What inspired you to do the film, 'Kallang Roar the Movie'?

CDA: Actually it was the Fandi era in 94 that inspired me. An entire nation was united behind our national football team then. But as soon as it came, it also went away as quickly, so I simply had to create a film that captured that spirit of the Kallang Roar. So I did my research and began my story in 1977 about a man who is absolutely passionate about achieving football success for his country.

RP: How did you do your research?

CDA: I quit every job I was doing. Back then I was just an intern for various film companies. So I put my focus on research and writing, and went to the old National Library daily to collect info. I also met up with some former national players to listen to what they have to say.

RP: Was it easy to find all your materials?

CDA: In addition to the National Library, I also went to Level 11 of the microfilm department of the Central Library next to Bugis Junction. I made a photocopy of practically every page in 1977 that had something to do with 'Uncle Choo' or local soccer. (Alas, I lent that research to someone and never got it back.)

RP: Why did you decide on Lim Kay Siu to play the role of 'Uncle Choo'?

CDA: Lim Kay Siu was a natural choice to play 'Uncle Choo'. As a person, he too was unafraid to speak his mind when it comes to the truth. As a professional actor, there was no one better or more qualified. The funny thing is I didn't know him personally. But what I did was set my mind to making him my lead, and I tried within all of my power to connect to him and I succeeded. I passed him the Kallang Roar script in Funan Centre, and the rest is history.

RP: Did you learn anything new about Uncle Choo?

CDA: In the course of making the film, both Kay Siu and I had to deepen our understanding of the man. He tried to achieve the impossible. He made his sacrifices. Sometimes in life, we can try so hard but we may not even succeed. So the final question is, even if you know you will most likely fail, would you have tried? For him, it was crystal clear; he loved football, so he would have done it anyway. He would have never stopped trying.

RP: What were his positive and not so positive qualities?

CDA: Positive: he was very headstrong, and very determined, and he would run through a brick wall to get to the finish line. Negatives: he was very headstrong, and that he ran through many brick walls to get to the finish line.

RP: How should Uncle Choo be remembered?

CDA: If you love football, if you love Singapore football, if you believe in Singapore football, cried over bad results of our national team, if you don't believe in naysayers or Facebook comments, if you believe that to make something happen is to work hard and find a solution rather than say that Singapore football will never succeed again, and also, if you believe that an honest and pragmatic approach (and not daydreaming) to improving Singapore football one step at a time is the answer, then 'Uncle Choo' is your hero and mentor.

Special interview with Lim Kay Siu
Lim Kay Siu played the part of Choo Seng Quee in the local hit movie, 'Kallang Roar the Movie'.

This interview was conducted via a questionnaire that I had sent to Lim Kay Siu on 19 December 2019.

RP — Reynold Pereira

LKS — Lim Kay Siu

RP: How did you get the role playing Choo Seng Quee in the film, 'The Kallang Roar'?

LKS: The Writer/Director, Cheng Ding An got in touch with me, and said to me that he had, *"a role for me that was unique, something I had never done before"*. So I met up with this totally passionate young man, who loved football so much, and had given up a dream of becoming a professional player through injury, and was going to embark on making his first-ever full-feature movie about the Singapore Lions under Choo Seng Quee. I was a real fan of the Singapore Team of that era, and Uncle Choo's infamy had really caught my imagination!

RP: How did you prepare yourself for the role?

LKS: All the research was done by Ding An. But on one occasion, he had invited some of the players of that amazing team, to meet up and talk about Uncle Choo!

The conversation was passionate, and Ding An and I could palpably feel the love they all had for this amazing man, who had, by now, passed away. There were tears shed, as they each piped in about how inspiring he was, and how much his tough love had changed their lives — and how he had stood up for them against some officious treatment from committee officials. And how he had never let them down when it came to welfare, even when the football body had refused what he thought as certain necessary aspects of welfare. He had come out with money from his own pocket.

They also marvelled at Uncle Choo's tactical brilliance — something they sometimes didn't understand, but trusted implicitly. They also described fondly how much he swore — something we could not include in the movie, because of Singapore-style censorship.

They also talked about his diabetes that eventually led to the amputation... his love for 'kueh lapis'... the tears flowed...

RP: You mentioned that you followed Singapore football during the 1970s. Did that help you in your preparation?

LKS: Very much so! I was a fan of that team — they were my heroes and Uncle Choo was a legend who I was enamoured with! I loved the fact that he swore so much!

RP: Were there any aspects of his character that you found difficult to portray?

LKS: I fell in love with this role, so every challenge was a welcome one. I always try to get into the humanity of the roles I play, but this was special.

RP: How was it to act alongside your real wife who played Uncle Choo's onscreen wife?

Swee Lin is such a good actor. She makes it look easy, and she establishes relationships so truly and so skilfully. It was a pleasure!

RP: Did you learn anything new about Uncle Choo?

LKS: How much love he inspired. Not just motivation and tactics, but love.

RP: What were his positive and not so positive qualities?

LKS: I believe he was a tough 'nut' when he was your adversary!

RP: How should Uncle Choo be remembered?

LKS: With respect, appreciation, and love. I think judging his swearing is petty.

RP: Any other comments you want to add?

LKS: I'm really grateful to Cheng Ding An for giving me the opportunity to play one of my heroes. With such humanity.

A Tribute from Quah Kim Song

Having played and managed football teams over the past 50 years, I fully understand the importance of having a good coach for a team. A coach can inspire a team to reach great heights and play above themselves. That is why I am especially pleased to be asked to write this short tribute to Choo Seng Quee. He was a pioneer of coaching and a visionary. Some of his ideas more than 50 years ago are being replicated by the teams and coaches of today.

I was spotted by 'Uncle Choo' (that's what many of us called him) as a 15-year-old while playing football in Farrer Park. I had already heard about him from by my brothers — Kim Beng, Kim Choon, Kim Swee, Kim Siak and Kim Lye — who had been coached by him. They warned me that he was a strict disciplinarian and a 'no-nonsense guy'. I was thus apprehensive and afraid. When I met him, he was larger than life, standing 6 foot 2. He had a reputation that was hard to match. He had been national coach of Malaysia and Indonesia before that, and achieved great success with those teams.

His successes with the Indonesian and Malaysian teams were no mean feat. He may not have won anything in terms of trophies with the Indonesian team. But they achieved remarkable success on their tours, most notably defeating three highly ranked Hong Kong professional teams.

With the Malaysians, he led them to a bronze medal at the 1962 Asian Games. Tunku Abdul Rahman, who was instrumental in bringing in Seng Quee, was prepared to do whatever it took to retain his services. This included sending him on a six-month coaching trip to the UK to further enhance his already immense knowledge of football tactics.

Though he had lucrative offers to continue with the Malaysian team, his heart was always with the Singapore team. He frequently offered his services to coach the Singapore team.

Sadly, his strong character and his reputation of wanting to manage teams his own way without interference from team officials resulted in him only having five short stints with the Singapore team. Each stint lasted only a year or so.

Yet, each time he was able to create a team capable of playing above themselves. His sometimes questionable training methods were not to everyone's liking but the results often proved themselves.

He also had a knack of creating multiracial teams which helped ease some of the racial tensions especially just after Singapore's separation from Malaysia in 1965.

I remember the starting line-up of the celebrated 1977 Malaysia Cup squad coached by Seng Quee had four Chinese, six Malay and two Indian players. Edmund Wee replaced a Eurasian keeper, Eric Paine.

His dedication to the game ironically also proved to be his downfall. While he was focussing his efforts on bringing home the Malaysia Cup in 1977, he ignored an infection resulting from a cut from a fall during a Malaysia Cup game. The infection turned gangrenous resulting in his right leg being amputated just below the knee.

Still, in spite of his amputated leg, he was still able to have one last hurrah, coaching the Johor state team in 1980. He died in 1983 after an illness.

Seng Quee worked tirelessly throughout his life to raise the level of the game in the teams he coached. His dedication to the game cannot be questioned. His knowledge of football as a coach was encyclopaedic, as he read extensively and did his research about football from other countries like England and Brazil.

I am glad that Reynold Pereira has taken on this ambitious project to write about this complex individual and to expose him to a newer generation of Singapore football fans. This is a great tribute to a true Singapore football icon.

Quah Kim Song
Ex-Singapore national footballer and ex-Chairman of
Tampines Rovers Football Club

Timeline

1914 — Birth of Choo Seng Quee

1983 — Passed away in his sleep at home

As a player

1930 — Played for Raffles Institution in the inter-school competition

1933 — Played for Singapore Chinese FA third team in the Third Division

1934 — Played for Singapore Chinese FA second team in the Second Division

1935–1939 — Played for Singapore Chinese FA first team in the First Division

1939 — Formed and played for Chinese Athletic (Chung Wah)

1940–1941 — Played for Hong Kong club Sing Tao

1946–1949 — Player/Coach for Chinese Athletic

As a coach

1949 — Elected honorary coach and adviser to the Hotspurs XI, a team of promising young Singapore footballers

1949 — Coach of Singapore Chinese FA

1949 — Coach of the Singapore FA for the Malaya Cup

1949–1953 — Coach of the Indonesian national football team

1952–1957 — Coach of Star Soccerites, a SAFA First Division team

1957 — Coach of Marine Department Sports Club, a SAFA First Division team

1958–1963 — Coach of the Malayan national football team

1964–1965 — Coach of the Singapore National football team

1968 — Coach of Police Sports Association

1968 — Coach of Singapore national football team

1971 — Coach of Singapore national football team

1971–1975 — Honorary coach of Burnley United, Singapore Marble, Tampines Rovers and Farrer Park

1973 — Rejected a coaching contract with Hong Kong professional club, Caroline Hill FC

1973 — Coach of West Irian State team on a two-month stint

1976–1977 — Coach of Singapore national football team

1980 — Coach of Johor State football team

Appendix 2

List of Achievements

C hoo Seng Quee has achieved so much in his long and illustrious career. No other coach in Asia could come as near to Seng Quee in terms of the impact on the rise of football in Singapore, Malaysia and Indonesia.

As a player
Singapore Chinese FA
SAFA Third Division Winners — 1933
SAFA Second Division Winners — 1934
SAFA First Division Winners — 1935, 1937, 1939

Singapore
Malaya Cup Winners — 1937, 1939

As a coach
Clubs
Star Soccerites
SAFA First Division Winners — 1954

Marine Department Sports Club
SAFA First Division Winners — 1957

Police Sports Association
President Cup Winners — 1968

Malaya
Merdeka Cup Winners — 1958, 1959, 1960
Merdeka Cup runners-up, 1961
SEAP Games Winners — 1961
Asian Games bronze medal — 1962
Merdeka Cup third place — 1962

Singapore
Aw Hoe Cup Winners — 1964, 1965, 1967
Malaya Cup Winners — 1965, 1966
Malaysia Cup Winners — 1977

Personal Honours
Singapore Coach of the Year — 1977
Pingat Bakti Masyarakat (PBM) — 1977
All Indonesian Soccer Federation (PSSI) First Class Gold Medal —
1980

International Coaching Statistics

The following are some statistics of Choo Seng Quee's international coaching career. He coached three national teams namely, Indonesia, Malaysia and Singapore.

Matches as coach of national teams

Total Matches	: 113
Won	: 42
Draw	: 19
Lost	: 52
Goals For	: 216
Goals Against	: 239
Wins Percentage	: 44.58%

Matches as coach of Indonesia

Total Matches	: 3
Won	: 1
Draw	: 0
Lost	: 2
Goals For	: 5
Goals Against	: 7
Wins Percentage	: 33.33%

Matches as coach of Malaya/Malaysia

Total Matches	: 70
Won	: 34
Draw	: 13
Lost	: 23
Goals For	: 168
Goals Against	: 120
Wins Percentage	: 57.86%

Matches as coach of Singapore

Total Matches	: 40
Won	: 7
Draw	: 6
Lost	: 27
Goals For	: 43
Goals Against	: 112
Wins Percentage	: 25.00%

Age First Match: 36 years 94 days 5-3-1951 vs. India 0-3
Age Last Match: 62 years 101 days 12-3-1977 vs. Hong Kong 0-1
National Team Career: 26 years 7 days

Coach for Indonesia

Caps	Date	Venue	Opponent	Score	Competition
1	5-3-51	New Delhi	India	0-3	Asian Games
2	9-3-51	New Delhi	Burma	4-1	
3	30-4-53	Hongkong	South Korea	1-3	

NB: unofficial international matches coached:

Date	Venue	Opponent	Score
18-4-53	Manila	Manila League	8-0
19-4-53	Manila	All Students XI	7-0
21-4-53	Manila	Manila Interport	5-0
25-4-53	Hongkong	Hongkong Interport	4-1
26-4-53	Hongkong	Hongkong Team	3-2
29-4-53	Hongkong	Chinese Combined	5-1
2-5-53	Bangkok	Chaisot	6-2
3-5-53	Bangkok	Thai Royal Air Force	7-0
26-8-53	Jakarta	Yugoslavia B	0-2

Coach for Malaya/Malaysia

<u>Malaya</u>

Caps	Date	Venue	Opponent	Score	Competition
1	1-3-58	Kuala Lumpur	Singapore	5-2	
2	2-3-58	Kuala Lumpur	Singapore	3-1	
3	3-5-58	Singapore	Singapore	3-3	
4	4-5-58	Singapore	Singapore	3-0	
5	14-5-58	Kuala Lumpur	Pakistan	4-2	
6	25-5-58	Tokyo	Taiwan	1-2	Asian Games
7	27-5-58	Tokyo	South Vietnam	1-6	Asian Games
8	4-6-58	Hongkong	Hongkong	2-2	
9	30-8-58	Kuala Lumpur	Indonesia	3-2	Merdeka Cup
10	1-9-58	Kuala Lumpur	Hongkong	3-0	Merdeka Cup
11	2-9-58	Kuala Lumpur	Singapore	0-0	Merdeka Cup
12	4-9-58	Kuala Lumpur	South Vietnam	2-0	Merdeka Cup
13	28-12-58	Kuala Lumpur	Japan	6-2	
14	4-1-59	Penang	Japan	1-3	

15	22-1-59	Rangoon	Burma	4-2	
16	24-1-59	Rangoon	Burma	2-3	
17	27-1-59	Rangoon	Burma	0-2	
18	11-5-59	Singapore	Singapore	5-2	Asian Cup Qualifier
19	13-5-59	Singapore	South Vietnam	0-1	Asian Cup Qualifier
20	30-8-59	Kuala Lumpur	South Korea	4-1	
21	2-9-59	Kuala Lumpur	South Vietnam	4-3	Merdeka Cup
22	4-9-59	Kuala Lumpur	India	1-1	Merdeka Cup
23	6-9-59	Kuala Lumpur	Hongkong	2-1	Merdeka Cup
24	13-12-59	Bangkok	Burma	2-1	SEAP Games
25	14-12-59	Bangkok	Thailand	1-3	SEAP Games
26	15-12-59	Bangkok	South Vietnam	2-1	SEAP Games
27	6-5-60	Kuala Lumpur	India	0-0	
28	5-8-60	Kuala Lumpur	Japan XI	3-0	Merdeka Cup
29	7-8-60	Kuala Lumpur	Thailand	8-2	Merdeka Cup
30	12-8-60	Kuala Lumpur	Pakistan	1-0	Merdeka Cup
31	14-8-60	Kuala Lumpur	South Korea	0-0 [1]	Merdeka Cup
32	28-5-61	Tokyo	Japan	2-3	
33	2-8-61	Kuala Lumpur	Japan	3-2	Merdeka Cup
34	5-8-61	Kuala Lumpur	South Vietnam	3-1	Merdeka Cup
35	9-8-61	Kuala Lumpur	India	1-2	Merdeka Cup
36	13-8-61	Kuala Lumpur	Indonesia	1-2	Merdeka Cup

37	23-10-61	Saigon	Indonesia	3-1	Vietnam Nat. Day
38	26-10-61	Saigon	South Vietnam	0-1	Vietnam Nat. Day
39	12-12-61	Rangoon	Cambodia	4-0	SEAP Games
40	13-12-61	Rangoon	Burma	2-1	SEAP Games
41	14-12-61	Rangoon	Thailand	2-2 [2]	SEAP Games
42	16-12-61	Rangoon	Burma	2-0	SEAP Games
43	26-8-62	Jakarta	Philippines	15-1	Asian Games
44	28-8-62	Jakarta	Indonesia	3-2	Asian Games
45	29-8-62	Jakarta	South Vietnam	0-3	Asian Games
46	1-9-62	Jakarta	South Korea	1-2	Asian Games
47	3-9-62	Jakarta	South Vietnam	4-1	Asian Games
48	8-9-62	Kuala Lumpur	Japan	2-2	Merdeka Cup
49	13-9-62	Kuala Lumpur	Burma	3-2	Merdeka Cup
50	16-9-62	Kuala Lumpur	Pakistan	0-0	Merdeka Cup
51	19-9-62	Kuala Lumpur	South Korea	3-1	Merdeka Cup
52	27-10-62	Saigon	Thailand	4-2	Vietnam Nat. Day
53	28-10-62	Saigon	Indonesia	1-2	Vietnam Nat. Day
54	30-10-62	Saigon	South Vietnam	0-2	Vietnam Nat. Day
55	8-8-63	Kuala Lumpur	Japan	3-4	Merdeka Cup
56	11-8-63	Kuala Lumpur	South Vietnam	0-5	Merdeka Cup

57	12-8-63	Kuala Lumpur	Taiwan	2-3	Merdeka Cup
58	14-8-63	Kuala Lumpur	Thailand	2-2	Merdeka Cup
59	16-8-63	Kuala Lumpur	South Korea	3-0 [3]	Merdeka Cup

[1] a.e.t. / trophy shared; regulation time was 2 × 40 minutes and extra time 2 × 5.

[2] a.e.t. / Malaya won on lots.

[3] Also reported as 3-2 to Malaya.

NB: *unofficial international matches coached:*

Date	Venue	Opponent	Score	Competition
6-6-58	Hongkong	Combined Chinese	5-2	
5-9-58	Kuala Lumpur	Rest of Merdeka XI	3-2	
5-10-58	Kuala Lumpur	Seoul FC	2-2	
13-5-61	Kuala Lumpur	England FA XI	2-4	
30-10-61	Saigon	South Vietnam XI	0-2	
26-5-62	Kuala Lumpur	British Army	4-3	
18-11-62	Kuala Lumpur	Sweden XI	0-0 [4]	
20-11-62	George Town	Sweden XI	0-4	
22-11-62	Kuala Lumpur	Sweden XI	0-1	
4-6-62	Kuala Lumpur	South Korea XI	1-3	
6-6-62	George Town	South Korea XI	3-4	
8-6-62	Alor Setar	South Korea XI	1-0	
21-9-62	Alor Setar	Pakistan	3-2	
23-9-62	George Town	Pakistan	1-4	
31-10-62	Saigon	South Vietnam Police	1-1	Vietnam Nat. Day
17-8-63	Kuala Lumpur	Commonwealth	3-1	Merdeka Cup

[4] abandoned in 17' due to heavy rain.

Malaysia

Caps	Date	Venue	Opponent	Score	Competition
60	12-10-63	Kuala Lumpur	Thailand	1-1	Olympic G. Qual.
61	16-11-63	Bangkok	Thailand	2-3	Olympic G. Qual.
62	7-12-63	South Vietnam	South Vietnam	3-5	Asian Cup Qualifier
63	11-12-63	South Vietnam	Thailand	3-1	Asian Cup Qualifier
64	14-12-63	South Vietnam	Hongkong	3-4	Asian Cup Qualifier
65	22-8-64	Kuala Lumpur	Thailand	3-0	Merdeka Cup
66	24-8-64	Kuala Lumpur	India	1-1 [5]	Merdeka Cup
67	28-8-64	Kuala Lumpur	Burma	0-3	Merdeka Cup
68	30-8-64	Kuala Lumpur	South Vietnam	1-2	Merdeka Cup
69	2-9-64	Kuala Lumpur	Taiwan	5-2	Merdeka Cup
70	5-9-64	Ipoh	Thailand	1-1	Merdeka Cup

[5] a.e.t. / India won by coin toss.

NB: *unofficial international match coached:*

Date	Venue	Opponent	Score
15-12-63	Saigon	S. Vietnam Civilians	2-1

Coach of Singapore (excluding Malaysia Cup games)

First tenure

Caps	Date	Venue	Opponent	Score	Competition
1	15-12-65	Kuala Lumpur	Burma	0-1	SEAP Games
2	16-12-65	Kuala Lumpur	South Vietnam	1-5	SEAP Games

Second tenure

Caps	Date	Venue	Opponent	Score	Competition
3	11-8-67	Kuala Lumpur	Taiwan	3-3	Merdeka Cup
4	13-8-67	Ipoh	Indonesia	1-4	Merdeka Cup
5	15-8-67	Ipoh	Burma	0-3	Merdeka Cup
6	20-8-67	Kuala Lumpur	South Korea	0-3	Merdeka Cup
7	4-11-67	Saigon	South Vietnam	0-2	Vietnam Nat. Day
8	8-11-67	Saigon	New Zealand	1-3	Vietnam Nat. Day
9	11-11-67	Saigon	Australia	1-5	Vietnam Nat. Day
10	21-11-67	Singapore	Australia	1-6	

Third tenure

Caps	Date	Venue	Opponent	Score	Competition
11	5-6-71	Jakarta	Indonesia	0-3	Jakarta Cup
12	9-6-71	Jakarta	Burma	0-6	Jakarta Cup
13	5-8-71	Kuala Lumpur	Hongkong	2-1	Merdeka Cup
14	7-8-71	Kuala Lumpur	Burma	1-0	Merdeka Cup
15	10-8-71	Kuala Lumpur	India	2-2	Merdeka Cup
16	13-8-71	Ipoh	Indonesia	0-4	Merdeka Cup
17	15-8-71	Kuala Lumpur	Philippines	4-4	Merdeka Cup
18	20-8-71	Kuala Lumpur	Malaysia	2-4	Merdeka Cup
19	23-8-71	Singapore	Malaysia	2-2 [1]	Pesta Sukan Cup
20	27-8-71	Singapore	Indonesia	3-2	Pesta Sukan Cup

21	28-8-71	Singapore	South Korea XI	1-4	Pesta Sukan Cup
22	28-10-71	Saigon	Thailand	0-1	Vietnam Nat. Day
23	30-10-71	Saigon	Malaysia	1-1 [2]	Vietnam Nat. Day
24	31-10-71	Saigon	Thailand	3-1	Vietnam Nat. Day
25	7-11-71	Bangkok	Thailand	0-2	King's Cup
26	9-11-71	Bangkok	South Vietnam	4-5	King's Cup
27	13-12-71	Kuala Lumpur	South Vietnam	1-3	SEAP Games
28	14-12-71	Kuala Lumpur	Burma	1-8	SEAP Games

Fourth tenure

Caps	Date	Venue	Opponent	Score	Competition
29	13-9-76	Seoul	Malaysia	1-4	President's Cup
30	15-9-76	Seoul	India	2-1	President's Cup
31	17-9-76	Seoul	South Korea	0-7	President's Cup
32	22-10-76	Singapore	Australia	0-1	
33	17-12-76	Bangkok	South Korea	0-4	King's Cup
34	19-12-76	Bangkok	Thailand	0-6	King's Cup
35	14-2-77	Singapore	South Korea	0-4	
36	27-2-77	Singapore	Thailand	2-0	World Cup Qualifier
37	2-3-77	Singapore	Hongkong	2-2	World Cup Qualifier
38	6-3-77	Singapore	Malaysia	1-0	World Cup Qualifier
39	9-3-77	Singapore	Indonesia	0-4	World Cup Qualifier
40	12-3-77	Singapore	Hongkong	0-1	World Cup Qualifier

[1] Singapore lost 4-5 on penalty kicks.
[2] Singapore lost 3-4 on penalty kicks.

NB: unofficial international match coached:

Date	Venue	Opponent	Score	Competition
24-8-67	Kuala Lumpur	Western Australia	3-5	Merdeka Cup

Total record

Matches	Won	Draw	Lost	For-Against	Points	Percentage
113	42	19	52	216-239	103	45.58

Types of matches

Merdeka Tournament	: 40
Friendlies	: 19
Vietnam Nat. Day Cup	: 11
SEAP Games	: 11
Asian Games	: 8
Asian Cup Qualifier	: 5
World Cup Qualifier	: 5
King's Cup	: 4
President's Cup	: 3
Pesta Sukan Cup	: 3
Olympic Games Qualifier	: 2
Other Tournaments	: 2
Total	: 113

Champions and Finalists for the Malaya/Malaysia Cup

Below are the list of champions and finalists for the Malaya/Malaysia Cup (Piala Malaysia) since its inception in 1921.

Year	Champions	Runners-up	Score	Venue
1921	Singapore	Selangor	2-1	Selangor Club Padang, Kuala Lumpur
1922	Selangor	Singapore	3-2	Selangor Club Padang, Kuala Lumpur
1923	Singapore	Perak	2-1	Selangor Club Padang, Kuala Lumpur
1924	Singapore	Selangor	1-0	Selangor Club Padang, Kuala Lumpur
1925	Singapore	Selangor	2-1	Anson Road Stadium, Singapore
1926	Perak	Singapore	1-0	Selangor Club Padang, Kuala Lumpur
1927	Selangor	Singapore	8-1	Selangor Club Padang, Kuala Lumpur

1928	Selangor & Singapore (trophy shared)		2-2	Selangor Club Padang, Kuala Lumpur
1929	Selangor & Singapore (trophy shared)		2-2	Selangor Club Padang, Kuala Lumpur
1930	Singapore	Selangor	3-0	Anson Road Stadium, Singapore
1931	Perak	Singapore	3-1	Chinese Assembly Hall, Ipoh
1932	Singapore	Selangor	5-3	Selangor Club Padang, Kuala Lumpur
1933	Singapore	Selangor	8-2	Rifle Range Road, Singapore
1934	Singapore	Penang	2-1	Selangor Club Padang, Kuala Lumpur
1935	Selangor	Singapore	3-2	Selangor Club Padang, Kuala Lumpur
1936	Selangor	Singapore	1-0	Rifle Range Road, Singapore
1937	Singapore	Selangor	2-1	Selangor Club Padang, Kuala Lumpur
1938	Selangor	Singapore	1-0	Selangor Club Padang, Kuala Lumpur
1939	Singapore	Selangor	3-2	Selangor Club Padang, Kuala Lumpur
1940	Singapore	Kedah	2-0	Selangor Club Padang, Kuala Lumpur
1941	Singapore	Penang	2-1	Selangor Club Padang, Kuala Lumpur
1942– 1947	Suspended due to the Second World War — Japanese occupation of Malaya, Singapore and British Borneo			

1948	Negeri Sembilan	Selangor	2-2 (2-1 pen.)	Selangor Club Padang, Kuala Lumpur
1949	Selangor	ATM	3-2	Selangor Club Padang, Kuala Lumpur
1950	Singapore	Penang	2-0	Selangor Club Padang, Kuala Lumpur
1951	Singapore	Perak	6-0	Selangor Club Padang, Kuala Lumpur
1952	Singapore	Penang	3-2	Chinese Assembly Hall, Ipoh
1953	Penang	Singapore	3-2	Chinese Assembly Hall, Ipoh
1954	Penang	Singapore	3-0	Selangor Club Padang, Kuala Lumpur
1955	Singapore	Kelantan	3-1	Rifle Range Road, Singapore
1956	Selangor	Singapore	2-1	Selangor Club Padang, Kuala Lumpur
1957	Perak	Selangor	3-2	Stadium Merdeka, Kuala Lumpur
1958	Penang	Singapore	3-3 (3-1 pen.)	Stadium Merdeka, Kuala Lumpur
1959	Selangor	Perak	4-0	Stadium Merdeka, Kuala Lumpur
1960	Singapore	Perak	2-0	Stadium Merdeka, Kuala Lumpur
1961	Selangor	Perak	4-2	Stadium Merdeka, Kuala Lumpur
1962	Selangor	Penang	1-0	Stadium Merdeka, Kuala Lumpur

Year	Team 1	Team 2	Score	Venue
1963	Selangor	Penang	6-2	Stadium Merdeka, Kuala Lumpur
1964	Singapore	Perak	3-2	Stadium Merdeka, Kuala Lumpur
1965	Singapore	Selangor	3-1	Stadium Merdeka, Kuala Lumpur
1966	Selangor	ATM	1-0	Stadium Merdeka, Kuala Lumpur
1967	Perak	Singapore	2-1	Stadium Merdeka, Kuala Lumpur
1968	Selangor	Penang	8-1	Stadium Merdeka, Kuala Lumpur
1969	Selangor	Penang	1-0	City Stadium, George Town
1970	Perak	Kelantan	2-0	Stadium Merdeka, Kuala Lumpur
1971	Selangor	Perak	3-1	Perak Stadium, Ipoh
1972	Selangor	Perak	3-0	Stadium Merdeka, Kuala Lumpur
1973	Selangor	Terengganu	2-1	Stadium Merdeka, Kuala Lumpur
1974	Penang	Perak	2-1	City Stadium, George Town
1975	Selangor	Singapore	1-0	Stadium Merdeka, Kuala Lumpur
1976	Selangor	Singapore	3-0	Stadium Merdeka, Kuala Lumpur
1977	Singapore	Penang	3-2	Stadium Merdeka, Kuala Lumpur

1978	Selangor	Singapore	4-2	Stadium Merdeka, Kuala Lumpur
1979	Selangor	Singapore	2-0	Stadium Merdeka, Kuala Lumpur
1980	Singapore	Selangor	2-1	Stadium Merdeka, Kuala Lumpur
1981	Selangor	Singapore	4-0	Stadium Merdeka, Kuala Lumpur
1982	Selangor	Terengganu	1-0	Stadium Merdeka, Kuala Lumpur
1983	Pahang	Selangor	3-2	Stadium Merdeka, Kuala Lumpur
1984	Selangor	Pahang	3-1	Stadium Merdeka, Kuala Lumpur
1985	Johor	Kuala Lumpur	2-0	Stadium Merdeka, Kuala Lumpur
1986	Selangor	Johor	6-1	Stadium Merdeka, Kuala Lumpur
1987	Kuala Lumpur	Kedah	1-0	Stadium Merdeka, Kuala Lumpur
1988	Kuala Lumpur	Kedah	3-0	Stadium Merdeka, Kuala Lumpur
1989	Kuala Lumpur	Kedah	2-1	Stadium Merdeka, Kuala Lumpur
1990	Kedah	Singapore	3-1	Stadium Merdeka, Kuala Lumpur
1991	Johor	Selangor	3-1	Stadium Merdeka, Kuala Lumpur
1992	Pahang	Kedah	1-0	Stadium Merdeka, Kuala Lumpur

1993	Kedah	Singapore	2-0	Stadium Merdeka, Kuala Lumpur
1994	Singapore	Pahang	4-0	Shah Alam Stadium, Shah Alam
1995	Selangor	Pahang	1-0	Shah Alam Stadium, Shah Alam
1996	Selangor	Sabah	1-1 (5-4 pen.)	Shah Alam Stadium, Shah Alam
1997	Selangor	Pahang	1-0	Shah Alam Stadium, Shah Alam
1998	Perak	Terengganu	1-1 (5-3 pen.)	Bukit Jalil National Stadium, Kuala Lumpur
1999	Brunei	Sarawak	2-1	Stadium Merdeka, Kuala Lumpur
2000	Perak	Negeri Sembilan	2-0	Shah Alam Stadium, Shah Alam
2001	Terengganu	Perak	2-1	Bukit Jalil National Stadium, Kuala Lumpur
2002	Selangor	Sabah	1-0	Bukit Jalil National Stadium, Kuala Lumpur
2003	MPPJ FC	Sabah	3-0	Bukit Jalil National Stadium, Kuala Lumpur
2004	Perlis	Kedah	1-0	Bukit Jalil National Stadium, Kuala Lumpur

2005	Selangor	Perlis	3-0	Bukit Jalil National Stadium, Kuala Lumpur
2006	Perlis	Negeri Sembilan	2-1	Bukit Jalil National Stadium, Kuala Lumpur
2007	Kedah	Perak	3-0	Bukit Jalil National Stadium, Kuala Lumpur
2008	Kedah	Selangor	3-2	Bukit Jalil National Stadium, Kuala Lumpur
2009	Negeri Sembilan	Kelantan	3-1	Bukit Jalil National Stadium, Kuala Lumpur
2010	Kelantan	Negeri Sembilan	2-1	Bukit Jalil National Stadium, Kuala Lumpur
2011	Negeri Sembilan	Terengganu	2-1	Shah Alam Stadium, Shah Alam
2012	Kelantan	ATM	3-2	Shah Alam Stadium, Shah Alam
2013	Pahang	Kelantan	1-0	Shah Alam Stadium, Shah Alam
2014	Pahang	Johor Darul Ta'zim	2-2 (5-3 pen.)	Bukit Jalil National Stadium, Kuala Lumpur
2015	Selangor	Kedah	2-0	Shah Alam Stadium, Shah Alam

2016	Kedah	Selangor	1-1 (6-5 pen.)	Shah Alam Stadium, Shah Alam
2017	Johor DT	Kedah	2-0	Shah Alam Stadium, Shah Alam
2018	Perak	Terengganu	3-3 (4-1 pen.)	Shah Alam Stadium, Shah Alam
2019	Johor DT	Kedah	3-0	Buki Jalil, National Stadium
2020	Cancelled due to COVID-19			
2021	Kuala Lumpur	Johor DT	2-0	Buki Jalil, National Stadium
2022	Johor DT	Selangor	2-1	Bukit Jalil, National Stadium

Appendix 5

Champions in Singapore

Singapore Amateur Football Association

1904 — Band & Drums (1st Battalion Manchester Regiment)

1905 — E Company (Sherwood Foresters)

1906 — Not played

1907/08 — Singapore Cricket Club

1908 — 2nd Battalion West Kentshire Regiment

1909 — 3rd Battalion Middlesex Regiment

1910 — 3rd Battalion Middlesex Regiment

1911 — Singapore Cricket Club

1912 — Singapore Cricket Club

1913 — King's Own Yorkshire Light Infantry

1914 — Singapore Cricket Club

1915–1920 — Not played

1921 — 1st Battalion South Staffordshire

1922 — 2nd Battalion Middlesex Regiment

1923 — 2nd Battalion Middlesex Regiment

1924 — Singapore Cricket Club

1925 — Singapore Chinese Football Association

1926 — 2nd Duke of Wellington's Regiment

1927 — 2nd Duke of Wellington's Regiment

1928 — 2nd Duke of Wellington's Regiment

1929 — Singapore Cricket Club

1930 — Singapore Chinese Football Association

1931 — Singapore Malays Football Association

1932 — Singapore Malays Football Association

1933 — Singapore Malays Football Association

1934 — Singapore Chinese Football Association

1935 — Royal Engineers

1936 — Royal Air Force

1937 — Singapore Chinese Football Association

1938 — Singapore Chinese Football Association

1939 — Singapore Malays Football Association

1940 — Royal Air Force

1941 — Royal Air Force

1942–1946 — Not played

1947 — Army

1948 — Rovers SC

1949 — Not played

1950 — Kota Raja Club

1951 — Tiger SA

1952 — Rovers SC

1953 — Tiger SA

1954 — Star Soccerites SC

1955 — Marine Department SC

1956 — Tiger SA

1957 — Marine Department SC

1958 — Darul Afiah FC

1959 — Darul Afiah FC

1960 — Indian Recreation Club

1961 — Chinese Athletic

1962 — Marines

1963 — Darul Afiah FC

1964 — Darul Afiah FC

1965 — Darul Afiah FC

1966/67 — Darul Afiah FC

Football Association of Singapore

1968 — Darul Afiah FC

1969 — Darul Afiah FC

1970 — Toto Pools SC

1971 — Guthrie Waugh

1972 — Armed Forces

1973 — Armed Forces

1974 — Singapore Air Transport-Workers' Union

NB: in 1975, the Football League was revamped from 118 clubs to 30.

Singapore National Football League

1975 — Geylang International

1976 — Geylang International

1977 — Geylang International

1978 — Singapore Armed Forces

1979 — Tampines Rovers

1980 — Tampines Rovers

1981 — Singapore Armed Forces

1982 — Farrer Park United

1983 — Tiong Bahru CSC

1984 — Tampines Rovers

1985 — Police SA

1986 — Singapore Armed Forces
1987 — Tiong Bahru CSC

FAS Premier League
1988 — Geylang International
1989 — Geylang International
1990 — Geylang International
1991 — Geylang International
1992 — Geylang International
1993 — Geylang International
1994 — Perth Kangaroos
1995 — Singapore Lions (national team)

S-League
1996 — Geylang United
1997 — Singapore Armed Forces
1998 — Singapore Armed Forces
1999 — Home United
2000 — Singapore Armed Forces
2001 — Geylang United
2002 — Singapore Armed Forces
2003 — Home United
2004 — Tampines Rovers
2005 — Tampines Rovers
2006 — Singapore Armed Forces
2007 — Singapore Armed Forces
2008 — Singapore Armed Forces
2009 — Singapore Armed Forces
2010 — Etoile FC
2011 — Tampines Rovers

2012 — Tampines Rovers
2013 — Tampines Rovers
2014 — Warriors
2015 — Brunei DPMM
2016 — Albirex Niigata (S)
2017 — Albirex Niigata (S)

Singapore Premier League
2018 — Albirex Niigata (S)
2019 — Brunei DPMM
2020 — Albirex Niigata (S)
2021 — Lion City Sailors
2022 — Albirex Niigata (S)

Cup Finals in Singapore

Year	Winners	Score	Runners-up
1892	Singapore Engineers	2-2	Royal Artillery
1892 (R)	Singapore Engineers	6-2	Royal Artillery
1893	Royal Engineers	1-0	Singapore Cricket Club
1894	10th Lincolnshire Regiment 1st	Shared*	10th Lincolnshire Regiment 2nd
1895	Royal Artillery	3-1	5th North Humberland Fusiliers
1896	5th North Humberland Fusiliers	2-0	Singapore Cricket Club
1897	1st Battalion The Rifle Brigade	4-0	Corporals of The Rifle Brigade
1898	12th Company Royal Artillery	3-2	West Yorkshire Regiment
1899	1st BKOR Lancaster Regiment	1-0	Tanjong Pagar FC
1900	12th Company Royal Artillery	0-0 1-0	35th Company Royal Artillery
1901	Singapore Cricket Club	3-1	12th Company Royal Artillery

1902	49th Company Royal Artillery	1-0	50th Company Royal Artillery
1903	Singapore Cricket Club	2-0	Fort Canning Recreation Club
1904	Harlequins	1-0	Manchester Regiment
1905	1st Battery Sherwood Foresters	1-0	Singapore Cricket Club
1906	1st Battery Sherwood Foresters	1-0	Singapore Cricket Club
1907	2nd Battery West Kent Regiment B	1-0	2nd Battery West Kent Regiment A
1908	2nd Battery West Kent Regiment	2-0	Royal Garrison Artillery
1909	3rd Battalion Middlesex Regiment	2-0	Royal Garrison Artillery
1910	3rd Battalion Middlesex Regiment	2-0	3rd Battalion Middlesex Regiment II
1911	The Buffs (East Kent Regiment)	1-0 [aet]	Wanderers
1912	The Buffs (East Kent Regiment)	2-1	Singapore Cricket Club
1913	1st Battalion KOYLI	2-1	Singapore Cricket Club
1914	1st Battalion KOYLI	0-0 1-0 [aet]	Singapore Cricket Club
1915– 1916	not played		

1917	1/4th Battalion KSLI	1-0	Singapore Recreation Club
1918–1919	not played		
1920	1st Battalion South Staffordshire	1-0	Singapore Recreation Club
1921	Singapore Cricket Club	2-1	Royal Engineers
1922	2nd Battalion Middlesex Regiment	1-0	Singapore Cricket Club
1923	2nd Battalion Middlesex Regiment	3-0	St Joseph's Old Boys
1924	HMS 'Pegasus'	2-1	Singapore Cricket Club
1925	Singapore Chinese FA	4-2	Royal Sussex
1926	2nd Bttl. Duke of Wellington's R.	2-1	Singapore Chinese FA
1927	2nd Bttl. Duke of Wellington's R.	6-1	Singapore Chinese FA
1928	2nd Bttl. Duke of Wellington's R.	4-1	Singapore Chinese FA
1929	Singapore Cricket Club	1-1 1-0	Singapore Chinese FA
1930	Singapore Malay FA	1-0	Welsh Regiment
1931	Singapore Malay FA	4-3	Gloucester Regiment
1932	Singapore Malay FA	1-0	Royal Air Force
1933	Wiltshire Regiment	5-3	Singapore Malay FA
1934	Singapore Malay FA	2-2 6-2	Marine Department
1935	Singapore Chinese FA	3-1	Singapore Malay FA

1936	Royal Artillery	2-0	Police
1937	Singapore Chinese FA Ist	2-2 3-1	Singapore Chinese FA IInd
1938	Royal Artillery	3-2	Royal Air Force
1939	Singapore Chinese FA	2-1	The Loyal Regiment
1940	The Loyal Regiment	1-0	Royal Air Force (Seletar)
1941	Royal Air Force (Seletar)	2-0	The Loyal Regiment
1942–1946	not played		
1947	Singapore Malay FA	2-0	Singapore Chinese FA IInd
1948	Kota Raja SC	3-0	Singapore Recreation Club
1949	Kota Raja SC	3-0	Base Ordinance Depot Civilians
1950	Royal Navy	2-1	Rovers SC
1951	Royal Navy	1-0	Kota Raja SC
1952	Tiger SA	3-0	Royal Air Force (Seletar)
1953	Tiger SA	2-1	Fathul Karib FC
1954	Rovers Sport Club	2-2 3-0	Royal Navy
1955	Marine Department SC	3-0	Argonauts
1956	Tiger SA	3-2	Marine Department FC
1957	Amicable AA	5-4	Indian RC
1958	Fathul Karib FC	3-1	Amicable AA

1959	Darul Afiah FC	3-2	Fathul Karib FC
1960	Royal Air Force (Seletar)	5-0	Fathul Karib FC
1961	Chinese Athletic	5-2	Royal Air Force (Seletar)
1962	Marines	3-2	Tan Tock Seng Hospital
1963	Tan Tock Seng Hospital	7-1	Junior AA
1964	Darul Afiah FC	3-1	Chinese Athletic
1965– 1967	not known		

*After 7 (*seven!*) matches were played and drawn, 11 players (3 from the first XI and 8 from the 2nd XI) had their names drawn out of a hat containing all 22 names to win the 11 available medals.

NB: according to a newspaper report on the occasion of the 1920 final, the winners (listed above) of the cups of 1896, 1900 to 1904, 1906, 1913 and 1917 were not inscribed on the trophy.

Abbreviations:
KOYLI = King's Own Yorkshire Light Infantry
KSLI = King's Shropshire Light Infantry

Football Association of Singapore President's Cup

1968/69	Police SA	3-2	Fathul Karib
1969	Royal Navy Wanderers	4-2 [aet]	Police SA
1970/71	Armed Forces	2-1	Police SA
1971– 1973	not known		

1974	Int'l Contract Specialists	1-1 [4-3 pen.]	Armed Forces
1975	Singapore Armed Forces	1-0	Tampines Rovers
1976	Geylang International	2-1	Farrer Park United
1977	Toa Payoh United	3-2	Geylang International
1978	Geylang International	4-1	Tampines Rovers FC
1979	Toa Payoh United	1-0	Tampines Rovers FC
1980	Police SA	5-1	Farrer Park United
1981	Farrer Park United	1-0	Changi Constituency
1982	Tiong Bahru CSC	3-2	Farrer Park Dynamos
1983	Farrer Park United	3-0	Singapore Armed Forces
1984	Singapore Armed Forces	1-0	Farrer Park Dynamos
1985	Tiong Bahru CSC	3-0	Geylang International
1986	Singapore Armed Forces	3-1	Police SA
1987	Tiong Bahru CSC	2-0	Police SA
1988	Jurong Town	3-2	Singapore Armed Forces
1989	Jurong Town	2-1	Police SA
1990	Geylang International	2-0	Singapore Armed Forces
1991	Geylang International	3-0	Singapore Armed Forces
1992	Balestier United	3-2	Geylang International
1993	not played		

Singapore FA Cup

1994	Tiong Bahru CSC	4-2	Geylang International
1995	Geylang International	2-1	Woodlands Wellington
1996	Geylang International	1-1 [4-2 pen.]	Singapore Armed Forces
1997	Singapore Armed Forces	4-2	Woodlands Wellington
1998	Tanjong Pagar United	1-0	Sembawang Rangers

NB: continued as amateur competition.

Singapore Cup (continuation of Singapore League Cup)

1998	Tanjong Pagar United	2-0	Singapore Armed Forces
1999	Singapore Armed Forces	3-1	Jurong
2000	Home United	1-0	Singapore Armed Forces
2001	Home United	8-0	Geylang United
2002	Tampines Rovers	1-0	Jurong
2003	Home United	2-1	Geylang United
2004	Tampines Rovers	4-1 [aet]	Home United
2005	Home United	3-2	Woodlands Wellington
2006	Tampines Rovers FC	3-2 [aet]	Chonburi (Province) FC
2007	Singapore Armed Forces	4-3	Tampines Rovers FC
2008	Singapore Armed Forces	2-1 [aet]	Woodlands Wellington
2009	Geylang United	1-0	Bangkok Glass
2010	Bangkok Glass	1-0	Tampines Rovers FC
2011	Home United	1-0 [aet]	Albirex Niigata (S)
2012	Singapore Armed Forces	2-1	Tampines Rovers FC

2013	Home United	4-1	Tanjong Pagar United
2014	Balestier Khalsa	3-1	Home United
2015	Albirex Niigata (S)	2-1	Home United
2016	Albirex Niigata (S)	2-0	Tampines Rovers FC
2017	Albirex Niigata (S)	2-2 [aet, 3-1 pen.]	Global Cebu FC
2018	Albirex Niigata (S)	4-1	DPMM (Brunei)
2019	Tampines Rovers FC	4-3	Warriors FC
2020–2021	not played (due to COVID-19)		
2022	Hougang United	3-2	Tampines Rovers

NB: Police FC (in amateur era Police SA) have subsequently undergone two name changes — Home United in 1997 and Lion City Sailors in 2020.

Geylang United were renamed to Geylang International in 2013.

Tiong Bahru are now known as Tanjong Pagar United.

Singapore Armed Forces FC are now known as Warriors FC.

FA Cup

NB: since 2001, the FAS has been organising a separate cup tournament for the amateur clubs (non-members of the professional league); the clubs from the professional league were excluded in the first five editions before gaining invitations (for their Prime League teams, a sort of reserves league) in 2006; this tournament is a continuation of the Singapore FA Cup held from 1996 to 1998 (which then included the professional league members).

2001	Andrew's Avenue	5-0	Tessensohn Khalsa Rovers
2002	Police SA	2-1	Singapore Cricket Club
2003	Tampines Rovers SC	3-1	Police SA
2004	Tampines Rovers SC	7-0	Katong SC
2005	Singapore Armed Forces SA	5-0	Tessensohn Khalsa Rovers
2006	Singapore Armed Forces FC (PL)	2-0	Singapore Cricket Club
2007	Geylang United (PL)	1-0	Singapore U-18 (PL)
2008	Singapore Armed Forces FC (PL)	1-0 [aet]	Katong FC
2009	Singapore Cricket Club	3-2	Balestier Khalsa (PL)
2010	Singapore Recreation Club	3-2 [aet]	Tampines Rovers (PL)
2011	Tampines Rovers (PL)	1-1	Singapore Recreation Club
2012	Balestier Khalsa (PL)	2-0	Siglap CSC
2013	Home United (PL)	4-1	Sporting Westlake FC
2014	Singapore Recreation Club	1-1 [aet, 5-3 pen.]	Balestier Khalsa
2015	Home United (PL)	5-1	Police SA
2016	Home United (PL)	3-1	Siglap FC
2017	Warriors FC (PL)	2-1	Yishun Sentek Mariners
2018	Yishun Sentek Mariners	3-1	Tiong Bahru FC
2019	Tiong Bahru FC	3-1	Yishun Sentek Mariners
2020–2022	not played (due to COVID-19)		

NB: Tampines Rovers SC (amateur) is a separate entity from Tampines Rovers FC (professional).

Singapore Armed Forces SA (amateur) is a separate entity from Singapore Armed Forces FC (professional).

Police SA (amateur) is a separate entity from Home United FC (formerly Police FC) (professional).

(PL) marks Prime League (which consists of reserve sides from the then S-League teams and national youth sides).

Singapore League Cup

1997   Singapore Armed Forces   1-0   Geylang United

NB: this tournament was renamed Singapore Cup in 1998.
Not to be confused with the 'new' League Cup inaugurated in 2007.

League Cup

NB: inaugural edition 2007; not to be confused with 1997 tournament.

2007	Woodlands Wellington	4-0	Sengkang Punggol
2008	Gombak United	2-1	Super Reds
2009	DPMM (Brunei)	1-1 [aet, 4-3 pen.]	Singapore Armed Forces
2010	Etoile	3-1	Woodlands Wellington
2011	Albirex Niigata (S)	0-0 [aet, 5-4 pen.]	Hougang United
2012	DPMM (Brunei)	2-0	Geylang United
2013	Balestier Khalsa	4-0	DPMM (Brunei)

2014	DPMM (Brunei)	2-0	Tanjong Pagar United
2015	Albirex Niigata (S)	2-1	Balestier Khalsa
2016	Albirex Niigata (S)	2-0	DPMM (Brunei)
2017	Albirex Niigata (S)	1-0	Warriors

NB: discontinued after the 2017 season.

(C) Copyright Erlan Manaschev, Jiri Tomes and RSSSF 1999/2018

Appendix 7

Winners of the Association Challenge Cup

1892 — Royal Engineers

1894 — Lincolns

1895 — Royal Artillery

1896 — Fusiliers

1897 — Rifle Brigade

1898 — RA

1899 — KO Regiment

1900 — 12th Company RGA

1901 — SCC

1902 — RA

1903 — SCC

1904 — Harlequins

1905 — Sherwoods

1906 — Sherwoods

1907 — B Team West Kents

1908 — West Kents

1909 — Middlesex

1910 — Middlesex
1911 — Buffs
1912 — Buffs
1913 — KOYLI
1916 — Shropshires

Acknowledgements

This book about Choo Seng Quee could not have been written without a great deal of help from many people. I am forever indebted to my cousin, Jerome Vaz, who first mentioned about this larger-than-life figure when I was only 10 back in 1974.

A big hi-five to my childhood buddy, Michael Seet, who was there from the start of this project and provided valuable feedback and managed to gather valuable information from some former football players especially R. Suria Murthi.

Special thanks to Hernaikh Singh for putting me in contact with World Scientific.

My thanks to Jiang Yulin, the editor at World Scientific, for his encouragement and support during the publishing stage.

I am also indebted to Lim Tien Jit (Rocky) who supported this project from the beginning and who put me in contact with many former Singapore football stars.

I am most grateful to the following former Singapore footballers for their valuable input: Lim Teng Sai, Robert Sim, R. Suria Murthi, Samsuddin Rahmat, Roy Krishnan, Lee Boon Meng, Ho Kwang Hock, Tohari Paijan, Jerry Fernandez, Brian Richmond and not forgetting Caroline Batchelor Kumar, wife of the late M. Kumar.

A big thank you to Justin Morais for his valuable input about life in Singapore in the 1950s and 1960s.

Special mention goes to Jita Singh and Seak Poh Leong for sharing their valuable experiences as a coach.

Thanks to film director Cheng Ding An and actor Lim Kay Siu for their thoughts on Choo Seng Quee.

Thank you, Danesh Daryanani for your editorial advice.

A shout out to Lim Peng Han for his valuable articles on the history of Singapore football.

Special thanks to Ko Po Hui for helping me obtain some articles from the National Library which were not available online.

Also, not forgetting Edmund Arozoo for his excellent touch-up work on some of the photos, and Syed Hassan Al-Mashoor for his advice on the book cover design.

A super big thank you to Quah Kim Song for his support and encouragement in this project and for writing the special tribute to Uncle Choo. Song, thanks for getting the book over the finishing line!

And finally, my wife, Karine for her love and support over the past 32 years, and my sons, Raphaël and Tristan. Love you all.

My humble apologies if I missed out on anyone. I will add your name in subsequent editions.

Any errors contained herein are mine and mine alone.

Bibliography

Books and Journals

Alcock, Charles William: Football: The Association Game (1906) (2018)

Aqwam Fiazmi Hanifan: Uncle Choo dan Latihan Fisik Timnas Era 1950 (Uncle Choo and National Team Physical Exercise 1950s) (2013)

Barr, Michael D.: Singapore: A Modern History (Bloomsbury Academic, 2020)

Braddell, Roland St. John: The Lights of Singapore (Methuen & Company, 1934)

Brooke, Gilbert Edward, Braddell, Roland St. John & Makepeace, Walter: One Hundred Years of Singapore: Being Some Account of the Capital of the Straits Settlements from Its Foundation by Sir Stamford Raffles on the 6th February 1819 to the 6th February 1919; Volume 1 (Andesite Press, 2015)

Brown, Edwin A.: Indiscreet Memories (Monsoon Books, 2007)

Emmanuel, Mark: The Malaysia Cup: Singapore and National Imaging in Singapore, 1965–1996

Horton, Peter A.: Shackling the Lion: Sport and Modern Singapore (International Journal of the History of Sport, 2002, Vol. 19, Nos. 2–3, 243–274)

Lim Peng Han: The Singapore Football League, 1904–1941: Towards the Institutionalization of Football in the Colonial Port City of Singapore (International Journal of the History of Sport, 2018, Vol. 35, Nos. 12–13, 1217–1237)

Lim Peng Han & Mohd Salleh Aman: The HMS Malaya Cup Football League, 1921–1941: Towards the Institutionalization of Football in British Malaya (International Journal of the History of Sport, 2017, Vol. 34, Nos. 17–18, 1981–2007)

Lim Peng Han & Mohd Salleh Aman: The Diffusion and Transmission of Football in the Straits Settlements and Malay States, 1874–1899: Early Inter-Settlement Games and Inter-State Competition Among European Clubs and Teams (International Journal of the History of Sport, 2018, Vol. 35, Nos. 12–13, 1335–1355)

Meisl, Willy: Soccer Revolution (Sportsman's Book Club, 1956)

Morse, Graham: Sir Walter Winterbottom: The Father of Modern English Football (John Blake, 2013)

Tan, Stewart: Urban Systems Studies: Planning for a Secure City (Centre for Liveable Cities, Singapore)

The Jalan Besar Heritage Trail (National Heritage Board, 2012)

Turnbull, C. M.: A History of Singapore 1819–1988 (Oxford University Press, 1989)

Wilson, Jonathan: Inverting the Pyramid (Bold Type Books, 2013)

Websites

eResources — A Singapore Government Agency Website at: https://eresources.nlb.gov.sg/main

Style Mesti Ada at: https://stylemestiada.wordpress.com

www.rsssf.com

www.fifa.com

Index